Short Story, verse, Commentary

Colin H Coles

ISBN 978-1-78792-000-2

Book design, layout and production management by Into Print
www.intoprint.net
+44 (0)1604 832149

Foreword

Sam Grant is the author, name for Colin Coles. Author attended **HMS *Conway*,** a former pre-sea training ship, and after two years training was accepted by Houlder Lines for a deck apprenticeship.

Author, just turned seventeen, boarded Motor Vessel **Shaftesbury,** in Newport and signed apprenticeship indentures for three years and three months.

Motor Vessel **Shaftesbury** was days away from sailing to South America with a full general cargo, which included lower hold cargoes of steel plate, crated machinery parts and medical equipment for a hospital. Tween-decks: decks with less depth and directly above main holds were stowed with single decker Leyland buses, lorry chassis, and a variety of bagged cargo which included bags of clear ICI polythene pellets, and China clay.

Three and four holds tween decks featured special cargo lockers, which could be secured and sealed when loaded with cases of whisky, spirits, liqueurs and large unblended barrels of whisky. Both number one and five holds were smaller than the three intervening ones, where ship narrowed at bow and stern. Lorry chassis' were wire secured either side of fore, and main deck holds. Red painted drums of ethanol, wire and dunnage strapped around the accommodation structure. Deck cargo attracted less shipping cost, where waves would break across both fore and main deck. Severe seas in the Bay of Biscay could test cargo stowed below decks**. Shaftesbury** experienced cargo breaking loose on one occasion, which required return to port to access damage and re stow, where appropriate.

Author completed his apprenticeship aboard a refrigerated cargo passenger liner. In each of author's three maritime novels vessel types have been adapted to accommodate descriptive narrative.

Fictional stories, but factual account of shipboard life brought into the telling of these three novels and also maritime sea stories and poems in this edition.

Short stories and verse, in this edition, written and composed while author has progressed with narrative of novels. There are short stories and poems of a maritime background, but do not comprise the majority of work.

Story, Verse and Commentary. Comprises.

Part One – Short Stories.

Part Two –Verse.

Part Three – Commentary choice.

Contents

Foreword   iii

Contents   v

Part One: Short stories

Winter in New Jersey   2

The Manor House   6

A Summer Fete   16

Venue for a Delegation   27

A Walk to Cranmere Pool   35

Postal Christmas Preparation (Circa, 1980)   40

A Renaissance Painting   43

Dingley Park School receives assistance from Foreign Office   47

Parthian Kinsman   51

Bramble Cottage   55

"Nyama"   63

Secret Cave   68

A Tray's Development   87

A Retail Chain Store   89

Part Two: Verse

All Thine   96

An Invitation: Eternal Love   101

A Life's Journey   102

Light and Darkness   104

Spirit of Spring   105

Waves   107
Stream Reveals Secret   109
We Meet – We Part – We Meet   112
Sea, Pebbles Sand   114
A Truth Machine – Automata to Supply   116
Autumn   117
Dreamtime – Aspects   119
Call of the Gulls   121
Tree   123
At Home in Lockdown   125
Green Growth Escape   126
Cargo Liner – Circa nineteen-sixties   129
Epic Poem: Mists of Time   131
Extract: character verse anthology.
Fictional, legendary, historical   148
Achillies: Trojan War Hero   148
Alice   152
Arthur   157
Beethoven   159
Boudica   162
Isambard Kingdom Brunel   164

Part Three: Commentary

Writing Routine   168
The Play's the Thing   171
Writing Topics   174
Retail Wisdom   176
A Beach Swim   179
Free Will, Choice, Coincidence   182

Part One: Short Stories

Winter in New Jersey

The ship's return to New Jersey was memorable in another way, that's apart from winter weather experienced. Proximity, to cold, made apparent, on entry to New York Harbour, where sizeable ice chunks could be seen floating down from the upper reaches of the Hudson. Even with head gear and ear muffs, it was bitterly cold, in that wheelhouse. Open bridge doors funnelled blasts of cold air in. Port side, a snow carpet lay on the coconut matted deck. Shoe imprints from First Mate, John Thirsk, disturbed fresh snow when he walked across the wheel house and out on to the portside bridge. Hands clasped, head raised, he called toward the Monkey Island, above

"Lookout – you can come down and keep watch here." Now, no need for a lookout, within the harbour, but he would be available to run errands. Captain Stevens, entered the wheelhouse, at this point and called out.~

'Shut down to half,' Mister, will you? Pilot's on the way.' In his hand, a typed message, with company logo, from the Radio Officer. Second and Third Mate were addressed as Mister, by Captain Steven's when they were on watch. A more emphatic **"Mr Mate,"** employed when the pilot or visitors were on board. A favourite question, I'd noted, was,

'Where are we Mister?' with arrival on the bridge, but not this time. For which, the officer of the watch needed to calculate distance run and give a position. A trick question, I'd decided, because Captain Stevens, used to walk the dividers along the pencilled course line, and establish the ship's estimated position himself, before asking the question.

John Thirsk, on hearing, the order, re-entered the wheelhouse, took hold of the electrically operated telegraph handle and switched it past half-speed and back into the half speed lock position, while calling out-

'Half speed, it is then.'

A delay of ten seconds followed before it ceased buzzing, which suggested that the Third Engineer was caught unawares, and not that near the control platform. I raised my eyes upwards, from the giro compass, to view a' boxed section of the new build Verrazano Narrows Bridge, which was moving out of view above. Twin wires reached, high in the sky, above the ship, across from Staten Island to Brooklyn. Over a nine-month voyage contract, each three-week gap between ship departure and return saw new construction development. Before the Humber bridge was built, this bridge was the largest single span in the world.

What made this trip from Tampico to Bayonne memorable? Apart, from the cold, and from the other six return visits? A major contribution was definitely that the crew had jumped ship two weeks earlier, enticed to stay ashore by the siren voices and company of Mexican senoritas, perhaps? That event, together with a first association with extreme cold, made arrival in Bayonne, memorable. I need to give some back story.

Back, in the tropical warmth of Tampico, the Bosun was sent into town, after cargo load by Captain Stevens to warn, the deck crew that he would leave without them, if they did not return immediately. This, to no avail. Bosun Jones was far too pleasant an individual for a ship's Bosun. A small, dapper, Welshman who wore a red and white spotted neck tie with neatly pressed denim jacket and jeans. Make no mistake, a valued crew member, in that he was a trained hairdresser.

Even, maybe a contributor to the crew being made welcome ashore, through their locks, being well shorn? But, in his day job, as Bosun, he was far too amiable to control this crowd (deck hands) on board, let alone ashore! The nature of the situation was revealed on his return, after he was sent to fetch the crew from a bar. He ran back, along the wooden dock, in open necked check shirt, best go ashore jeans and polished brown shoes, waving his arms. The boat deck was no more than fifteen feet above and when he caught sight of Captain Stevens, Bosun Jones stopped with his right arm held up and gave a hand wave, much like you would wave to a friend's departure, whilst on a train platform. A wave which, seemed inappropriate, given the situation.

'Captain, Captain,' he called out. We, that's Peter, the junior apprentice and myself were close to where the Bosun was, at main deck level and could hear gasps and gulps, as he gathered himself, for another attempt, which was started but interrupted by Captain Stevens's, call back,

'What is it Bosun?' A reply in a deep, relaxed, but also impatient voice.

'Captain, Captain – they're not coming back.'
'Do you want to stay then Bosun?'
'No, Captain, but they won't leave the bar.
'Well, you'd best get on board then.'

Stewards, the galley boy and two junior engineers, assisted in letting go the ships lines, and winching them aboard.

With only the deck boy and Bosun on board, it meant Peter and myself did virtually turn and turnabout, in steering the ship back to New Jersey.

Once, tied up alongside, rat guards***** fitted to lines ashore, covers lashed on lifeboats, and a Venezuelan courtesy flag hoisted, I stood down until the midnight deck watch.

At about ten, next morning, I was on deck when three yellow cabs, appeared at the end of the jetty, having foolishly grabbed a metal stair rail, glove less and with temperature drop, severe enough to hand freeze, skin was ripped from palm of said hand. Tiredness, seeped into the eyes at the end of each watch, and it became understandable, how falling asleep could lead to hypothermia, in such conditions. The yellow cabs? They were the twelve returning crew members, flown back from Mexico.

Captain Stevens, called out,

'Welcome aboard lads.' They were logged a month's pay to cover costs, but didn't appear disgruntled by this. Most said it was well worth it, and were in better spirits, than before.

* Rat Guards: Full circle shaped – aluminium discs, which came apart to straddle ropes. A dog collar protective effect to prevent rats leaving the ship, along a sagging sisal rope or wire spring. Port authority regulations for ships berthed at a dock. An international requirement to help prevent rat infestation in dock yard premises.

The Manor House

Rivulets, streamed down tree trunks, breaking into a quiet, decayed, stillness of that wood. Ravaged elm trees, forlorn, like some bombed out town. I walked towards the Manor House, seeking immediate shelter, as much as a bed for the night. I'd asked previously at the station about booking office accommodation.

"Phone Mrs Batchem, at the Manor, she takes in guests – minding it for the Colonel, she is. There's nowt else here for bed and breakfast,' said the ticket collector at Ucklesbury station. I enquired on my mobile from Dunroamin cottage. This particular deceased client's inventory would need time to complete.

'That's quite right, but you won't mind the grand-children. They'll be a-bed afore you, no doubt,' said Mrs Batchem. I booked there and then. The bank would re-imburse. Now as I walked out of the dead elm forest, the three-story Manor loomed in front. The word Manor twinned with House on the adjacent gate post.

Rain from guttering, tumbled into the garden. I tugged the oval metal handle, which made a bell clang repeatedly. Patter of footstep followed. A thud of top and bottom bolts opening. The door, on opening, caught on a chain. I leant forward and said,

'It's Mr Stevens. I booked earlier.'

'Mr Stevens, I've been expecting you.' A pointed nose retreated.

The door bolt released. I was first to speak.

'It's very good to put me up at short notice. It's a filthy evening.'

'That's quite all right. Maurice from the station, let me know, you would be wanting – bed and breakfast,' she said, and fully opened the door. Mrs Batcham wore a navy skirt, matching coat and white blouse. Long black hair teamed up with hooped golden ear rings. She smiled.

'Do come in, won't you?'

The lines around her eyes merged with prettily etched cheeks. Friendly and welcoming. I guess mid-forties.

'There's a fire in the drawing room. The Colonel never lights the fire, except for guests. You'd like tea and sandwiches, perhaps? Cheese and chutney or just plain cheese?

'Cheese and chutney sounds good.' I had downed a pie and pint at the White Hart, not expecting food, but pleased to be offered tea and sandwiches.

'I'll show you your room Mr Stevens. The bath rooms opposite. We'd best go quietly-the grand children are asleep.' I followed her upstairs. She turned the Yale key in the bedroom door, removed it and gave it to me. I walked over and placed my suitcase and laptop on a high-backed chair by the bedroom window. A double room with wardrobe, chest of drawers. Two silver candle sticks stood on a mantelpiece, which faced a double bed.

'Fifteen minutes and I'll have the tea and sandwiches ready.' She smiled and closed the door.

Sun faded blood red wallpaper was disturbed, more than decorated with pictures of the highlands. Above, a black marble mantelpiece could be seen imprint from a slim object, which had been removed, to leave a dark curved strip. I considered asking about this, but Mrs Batchem did most of the talking.

'How very interesting, Miss Simkins used to visit the shop

for a quarter of hum-bugs, every week. I help at the post office you see Mr Stevens. But she didn't stop by a few weeks back. Died in the garden, she did. You know, the postman couldn't get an answer when he called with a parcel. He told us, he'd try the following day. He still couldn't get an answer. Sal, the postmistress first phoned the doctor. With no reply he had Sal call the police. They found her body in the back garden. A set of shears were locked in a branch, and she was lay nearby on the ground. A keen gardener. Died doing what she enjoyed, you might say.'

'That explains the new set of keys the bank gave me,' I said. I considered that I might as well explain why I was in Ucklesbury. It wasn't a state secret that I did bank inventories for deceased clients with no living relatives.

I've to get the grand children's clothes ready, you'll have to excuse me. The remotes by the TV and there's the Ucklesbury Times if you are wanting some local news.

'Thanks Mrs Batchem.' The carriage clock, stridently interrupted, before I continued.

'I started early from Paddington. I won't be long for bed. What's the Wi Fi like?

'There's a card behind the clock.' She pointed towards it, and I stood up and found a white calling card with a number written in biro.

'Be sure to replace it, won't you? I do breakfast for eight-thirty. A full English is that all right?'

'That's great, Mrs Batchem.'

'Will you be wanting tea or coffee Mr Stevens, which would you prefer, tea or coffee?'

'There's orange juice.'

'Black coffee will be fine,' I said.

'Will you be needing a call?'

'No, it's okay, I'll set my phone to wake me.'

'Modern technology does so much now, doesn't it? She replied. 'I'll wish you a good night's sleep then.'

I messaged the bank with an update on progress. My eyes closed momentarily, long enough to startle me on waking, expecting to see the furniture of my own lounge. It was definitely time for bed!

A walk upstairs, removed the sleep drug effect. I brushed my teeth in the bath room. Once in bed I accessed photos from Becky. They were sent from the Norwegian fjords aboard a cruise ship. We'd met on a bank course. I asked her out on my thirty ninth birthday. Last week, I turned forty. An instant attraction. She insisted it cooled. Although separated from her husband she wanted the divorce to be finalized. I was comforted to see in the selfies and photos featured just her and Millie, a former school friend. Mainly the two of them with scenic views of the fjords as a back drop – it was no good, I needed sleep and connected the I-pad to a charger. Returned to bed and set my phone to give a jingle at seven forty-five. The old feathery type mattress, wrapped itself around me.

I was dreaming, when I first realized that there was someone or something in the room. I felt to be awake. That was the strangeness. I was aware of being unable to move, lay on my back, but managed to move my arms, backwards in the dream, to raise my back.

At the front of the black mantelpiece, in my dream state, a young woman, appeared, in a pocketed tartan cape, over a white night dress.

Candles flickered at each end of the mantle piece. Black tresses curled around her shoulders. Hair highlighted by a white night dress.

Above the mantelpiece that strip of bright red wallpaper

now covered with a dirk in its scabbard. I was attracted by the raw beauty, but her face was one of anger. I could see the whites of her eyes around the coal black sparkle of pupils, which sought recognition. A look, full of anger, directed towards me. Yes, I now know, it surely was only a dream but I felt the full force of her wrath. Frozen with fear and in that dream capture I felt trapped.

She turned, withdrew the dirk from its scabbard. I felt a searing pain in my stomach, as she lunged forward. The cockerel crowing from a nearby farm made anger turn to disappointment on her face. The pressure of the dirk in my flesh went and her life size figure shrank. It seemed to fade back into the mantle piece. Now awake; equally captivated by the ravishing beauty of the young woman and terrified at the same time.

At breakfast 'You, can't have my phone to play games on, it's not my fault you left yours on charge at home.'

'Gran, isn't she mean. Sara's not using her phone. It's upstairs in the bedroom.

'When you've finished breakfast, you can both go into the orchard and play clock golf. Your mother's picking you up soon. It'll be your last chance.' It went quiet and the green baize door opened moments later. Mrs Batchem carried my breakfast in on a tray.

'Did you sleep well Mr Stevens? I meant to ask.' I wasn't sure whether the grand children were in hearing range and said,

'I went to sleep straightaway.'

'Dunroamin cottage's nearby,' She placed the tray on the sideboard.

'Yes, that's fortunate. Although it would be nice if the rain stopped.

'Is the manor old?' She placed my breakfast down and

went to fetch the tray with the coffee from the side board.

'I should say so. Built 1815, just after the Battle of Waterloo.'

'Old enough to produce a ghost I would imagine.' I was fishing to discover more.

'There's Annie MacBride. But I've neither seen nor heard her. My grandchildren. You know children Mr Stevens; they have wild imaginations. They've said that they've heard footsteps across the landing. Young Sara has said she saw a young woman in a tartan cape and night dress when she came down to get her phone. They watch so many films. It's all in their imagination, I'm sure. I've not told them the story, though about Annie. The Colonel, said there was the ghost, called Annie before he left. I do wish he hadn't. That started them off. Any unusual noise they've since heard has been Annie! It's all in their minds, Mr Stevens.'

'What do you know about Annie, Mrs Batchem?' I heard a scream from the kitchen.

'You dare, Justin. Give me back that charger.'

'Perhaps, after breakfast, I can tell you more. Sara and Justin need keeping an eye on. That's if you don't mind joining me around the kitchen table. I'll need to watch them from there

'Yes, I'd like that,' I said. She smiled and left for the kitchen.

'You two – Justin give Sara her charger, and both of you can put your shoes on and play in the orchard for half an hour.' I later carried the tray from the dining room to the kitchen.

I placed the tray on the kitchen table. A square oak table with the end leaves down.

'Thank you. Do sit down, won't you,' she said. I sat opposite. Not an elaborate kitchen. The ivory painted walls were cupboarded both sides of the Aga, which was built into an inglenook, beneath a large mantle piece. A faded portrait of a young woman in fine clothes looked down. The eyes looked familiar. The washing machine and dish washer seemed somehow futuristic beneath a drying frame that hung from the ceiling.

'I don't have many guests. It's nice talking with the outside world, you might say.' Mrs Batchem, sipped her tea, elbows on table.

'I'm Alice – an old-fashioned name. Alice was the name of mother's favourite teacher.'

'Brandon's my name. There was a Canadian great uncle on my father's side with that name. I was called All Bran at school.' She smiled, perhaps in memory of her schooldays. I'd ventured pass the threshold of just a paying guest.

Alice continued by telling me about Marge or Margie, the previous housekeeper. A boisterous individual, who apparently gave womanly advice to the Colonel, but winkled out of him the connection of Annie MacBride with the Manor. Then, his wife left him for a younger man, and Alice said that Marge made it clear that unless he found another wife she would leave as well.'

'And did he?' I asked Alice, who told me that he wasn't making much progress until Marge got him on a dating website. I then asked whether Marge was interested. Alice laughed and said that she wouldn't be - not with a female partner! But Marge, Alice said, wasn't impressed with his choice of women. He wanted to date single mothers with children. Alice, was surprised that any young woman would want him, but she said that next month he was going on a family outing to Alton Towers with a woman called Anita, and her two children. Marge said that she decided to leave, because she couldn't stand children. That didn't bother Alice.

Now that her daughter's children were at school, she would see less of them and didn't mind it if there were children at the manor. I wanted to know more about Annie. According to Alice there existed only rumours, before Marge got the story out of the Colonel.

Annie, apparently travelled down from Scotland with her Laird, in eighteen ninety. The then Laird was great uncle to the Colonel. There was a coachman, but no other servants. The Laird's wife died, and he acquired a mistress. Annie was her maid servant and the Laird fell for her and she for him. Annie arrived at the Manor, first as his maid servant. Alice said, that she would have been like his chattel or property. Marge, Alice said was of the belief that it would not have been a love match, but just plain lust for a younger woman. The Manor House was his English retreat and staffed with servants, who awaited their Laird's appearance. Apparently, Annie, was in servants' dress, but that the Laird gathered the staff and told them that Annie MacBride was to be their new mistress.

Fine clothes were bought. She liked to wear tartan, a statement of her Highland ancestry. That it was likely to have been difficult for Annie. Her romantic attachment to their Laird, would have upset staff at the manor. A maid servant becoming the mistress! I asked Alice whether they did get married. That appeared to be the plan. Alice said that according to Marge she wore an engagement ring. The Colonel said, it was afterwards given to his mistress. I questioned the fact that the Laird would want to marry a servant girl, but apparently, he did. A letter arrived, continued Alice, stating that she wanted him to return to Scotland. Annie was to stay at the Manor. The mistress now had a new maid servant. But, of course knew nothing of how Annie was bride to be. Alice then said how tragic it was with the name Mac Bride, but also that it was believed that Annie read the message before-hand. When he told her that he would be returning to the Highlands on business, she questioned this. They argued. It was said the servants over-heard the two rowing, but the coach man was told to prepare the coach and horses. Marge told Alice that the Colonel told her that there was a great stillness in the house and that the moon became red in the sky. I asked what happened and this is what Alice said.

'That the details are still not fully known, but the coach man drove the coach from the coach house around, and into the driveway, early that next morning. The Laird's belongings were packed and he said that they would stop and breakfast at The Old Red Lion in Tewkesbury.'

'Was it the main entrance where it says – Manor House?' I asked.

'Yes, that would be it,' she replied. Alice continued,

'The horses reared up as the coach approached. It was near to dawn. He reined them in and got down and there face down on the cobbles was Annie. It is said that there was blood down her night dress, but that she was breathing. He opened the coach door picked her up and placed her inside. Then went to waken the then housekeeper. When she saw Annie in the coach, she said to take her to the hospital, such was the amount of blood and that she would stay in the coach with her.' Alice's face whitened as she recalled the story, but continued.

'The coachman recalled that there was a terrible moaning from Annie. Her head was bloodied and once at the hospital they got help to take her inside. The two of them waited by the coach and shortly afterwards the nurses came out and said that she died in their arms. On their return to the manor, it was decided that the coach man, should go to the Lairds bedroom to wake him. He was met with the horrendous sight of the Laird lay across the bed with a dirk in his middle. The sash window wide open and each curtain had blood hand prints on them.'

I wanted to know more about the Laird, but Alice, Mrs Batchem continued.

'Evidently, if Annie couldn't have him neither would the mistress. The coroner determined death by suicide, while the mind was disturbed, for poor Annie. It was a double-edged dirk. Marge could have left the gory details out, but it was his blood on the nightdress. There was blood and more in the pockets of the cape. The blow to the head might have killed her, but it was not that severe and actual cause of death was listed as heart failure. Margie, said that Annie's ghost might be expected to appear, given the tragic circumstances. But she said no woman has been known to see her ghostly form. I don't want to believe that she's appeared to Sara. The Colonel's in his seventies, but he's never seen or heard anything that might be Annie's ghost. He just jokes about it. You might say that it's no more than a story. Not really history. It would not surprise me if it was all made up. Margie might have made it up to scare me even!'

'How old was the Laird, Alice? Was that mentioned?'

'Not an old man. He was just turned forty. There's a picture of him in the Colonel's private living room. Underneath, in the faded gold frame in black paint there's a plaque. It states: Born 1850 Died 1890. Previously engaged to Annie Mac Bride.

Poor man. He died two weeks after his fortieth birthday.' I realized that, I was exactly the same age.

Author grew, up in a seaside town. Part of a family, who were keen yachtsmen and women. Story builds, an imaginary setting where a newcomer joins a dinghy club, who previously sailed on an inland reservoir. Race, national championships were held in the town and the "sea," in all its vagaries, could visibly be seen to be a challenge to these "lake," rather than "sea," dinghy sailors. Sam Grant's story picks up from author's memories, when a child, in the nineteen – fifties, of a yacht club fund raising activity. A fund-raising fete was held, with similar outcome. Characters described are fictional, as is the story.

A Summer Fete

I will introduce myself. At the time in my late thirties, with a background of national service, not exactly green under the gills. With name of James Wilkes, quickly converted to Jim, by most friends and acquaintances. Although, to older family relatives I remained James. Transfer to the south coast by my company meant I could pursue an interest in sail boat racing to a new level, at Boscombe Yacht Club. Previously, sail club racing was a hut and a gravelled dinghy park. Sailing experience was limited to an inland lake which belonged to a landowner. Treated, at the time of the summer Fete with some suspicion by local members of Bascombe Yacht Club. Their spacious club house overlooked a beach popular with swimmers in the summer. I was there, I recall because with that keenness to find acceptance had said "yes," to the role of social secretary at the AGM. With a membership of over one thousand, shepherded by Vice Commodore Chris Wainwright, on a visit to the clubhouse. Unlike corporate organizations there were no photographs of executive officer members on walls. I was in those colloquial terms very much a furriner.

'Meet Jim. He's just told me that he used to race Flying Fifteens in a swimming pool-that's right isn't it' Jim?' I smiled, good humouredly, mainly because Chris was the Vice Commodore. A grizzled old timer further down the bar, made comment.

'Got a lot to learn about tides.' He continued in sarcastic manner.

'How to manage waves? You'll have not raced in a force five.' His friends around the bar nodded.

We raced on a reservoir. I suppose it was like a lake,' I said. 'I'm learning to cope.' Up until now I'd not ventured into the club house. My previous sail club rented the village hall for social events. This club house, with bar, lounge and billiards room was shabby, but the pictures of "J" Class yachts on the walls of the stairway recalled grandness. The butler and footman to the owner, would likely have been crew members.

An owner who would employ his own sailmaker and carpenter. I might have been a crew member, a generation back, but not a member of this club. Now, if you owned a boat with a mast and sail the committee were keen to have your membership fee. But I was not at the club house, for the subsidized beer. I was now the social secretary and felt that I should be visible to members from time to time. Julie my crew member seconded the proposal made. I'd just about forgiven her.

'Don't take too much notice of old Bill. He talks the talk you might say, Jim, but he's an arm chair yachtsman,' said

Chris. 'By the by very impressed with your fund-raising idea for a garden party at beginning of September.'

'Thanks,' I said.

'You know the story, don't you? About the need for a new start platform?'

'Not sure,' I said. I decided to be politic and pretend that I didn't. With my Guinness pored we left the bar to sit where chairs overlooked the harbour.

"Holidaymaker killed on beach with race gun." – were the Herald's headlines and the editor a member! Said Chris. He continued to explain.

'Our race gun was fired from the club house and a holidaymaker, asleep in his deck chair, coincidentally died of a heart attack. It read like he'd been shot – such rubbish! A race ten-minute gun just happened to be fired. His wife saw that he was having difficulty breathing and CPR was tried, but he was dead on arrival at hospital. The coroner reported that he had an existing heart condition and with the amount of alcohol, plus the strong sun. Conditions in place for a heart attack. No mention of the start gun! All thanks to that headline the damage was done, Jim. We received a letter from the Town Clerk that to continue with sail boat racing the start platform would need to have its gun fired away from the beach area and noise was hitting ice cream sales on the beach. Where do they get the nonsense from?'

We've got a plot of land overlooking the bay, but that's where the Garden Party comes in. A work force to build the hut – no problem, but we need cash to buy materials and electrical fittings. You're chairing a meeting next week to get things started, I understand.

'Yes,' I said.

I got straight to the point at that meeting mentioned by Chris.

'Does anyone know of a sail club member with a really large garden-suitable for our garden fete?' Stan Wilkins, who assisted with boat maintenance, raised a hand.

'Mr Chairman.'

'Yes Stan.' Pockets of meet and greet talk, were in progress around the table.

'Listen up,' I raised my voice to get attention and once the chat subsided said. 'Please continue. Stan.'

'There's the Stewarts' Mr Chairman. They help out aboard Jalopy Jane (Guard boat). Mrs Stewart said that she'd heard about the council's decision to ban the start gun from the beach and that we needed a new place, and she said wished that she could help. They've a sizeable lawn and smaller one. Cherry trees give some shade. Ideal space for tents and stalls. Sheltered from the road, you see. Can ask Mrs Stewart, Mr Chairman I go around to tidy up the garden. She'd be the one to ask. The Colonel's putty in her hands.'

'Much appreciated, Stan, if you'd do that. Sounds that they might be able to help. Folk love to visit other peoples' houses and gardens. This got the ball rolling and Dave Trant, supplier of fairground stalls and attractions came in with,

'I'll help out with supply of stalls and child rides, if the club can find members willing to assist with the labour. This was great news.

'That's most generous of you Dave,' I said. Others offered help. Marcia, a social member said that she could give palm and tea leaf readings for two shillings. One of which could go to the start race hut fund. Provided a tent could be provided.

'Thank you, Marcia,' I said. 'That will add some mystique to the proceedings.'

Others suggested raffles. A numbered entrance programme with a top prize of a family ticket to several seaside shows was agreed upon to appeal to holidaymakers.

'We need someone of note to open the fete, don't we?' said Vice Commodore Chris. The Herald's editor, Ian Hurst, in an attempt to redeem himself said, in the presence of members.

'I can likely get Dick West, local tele presenter to cut the tape. Herald will meet his fee, provided we get a mention, you understand.' This led to clapping and possible elimination of previous animosity directed toward Ian for his damaging headline. I looked at Chris, who gave me a thumbs' up. As Vice Commodore, he oversaw expenditure.

Apart from Marcia's Tarot reading, there was to be a magic spinning arrow, although how magic was involved was hard to see. The arrow revolved around a table of forty numbers. A prize given for the number it stopped at. A large open tent for a coconut shy and a crazy kitchen. Dressers stacked with crockery seconds, for punters to throw wooden balls at. It was suggested that this activity would appeal to housewives. Candy floss, popcorn, vanilla and strawberry ice cream. Both cornets and wafers. Plus, a couple of army surplus tea urns. Bottles of Camp Coffee available for the few who might prefer coffee. A tombola stall with pink and yellow raffle ticket numbered prizes. Prizes donated by members plus some funded from committee funds. Members donations were mainly back cupboard items, like tinned tapioca, stewed prunes, spaghetti and corn beef or spam. Premium prizes were boxes of chocolates, jars of sweets and half bottles of gin and whisky. Many everyday items were sought after with rationing still not fully over with from the war years.

At the end of the meeting, I said.

'It's looking good. Let's hope next Tuesday, I can bring back some news about a garden venue.' – "Meeting adjourned."

There was a race on Wednesday and Julie my crew, a florist said that she took a nosy look at the garden after delivery of flowers to Edenhurst. I'd said that Stan was sounding Mrs Stewart out.

'It's a two-tiered garden,' she said. 'A path circles front of the house. Then there're steps down. Two paths at each end lead to the lawns. It's rather grand,'

'Not too grand to hold a sailing club garden party?

'Will there be a yacht?'

'Not a bad idea. We could a have one rigged on a trailer. It might encourage new members.'

It would be great if Colonel and Mrs Stewart could open their garden for a fete.'

'Will you being going if we get it sorted?' I asked.

'Maybe,' she said. When is it?'

'First Saturday in September.'

On Thursday, Mrs Stewart called me at home, after a gardening visit from Stan.

'Could I manage afternoon tea on Saturday.' There was no cricket so I said "yes."

On arrival, I pressed the bell to the outer door and heard chimes sound further into the building. She struggled with the front door and I assisted with a push. The door gave up its fight to stay shut and I fell forward She grabbed my shoulder and laughingly said.

'We really must get this seen to. So good of you to come around, James.' Mrs Alexandra Stewart was a young woman in her late twenties whom I'd assumed to be the Colonel's daughter or niece when I saw her with Colonel Stewart on the guard boat.

21

'Reginald's in the garden, but do come in, won't you?'
A thirty-foot hall with a reception area to one side fronted
three doors and a stairway. A corridor by its side led to the
kitchen further down. I tried not to look awestruck by its
spaciousness.

'We mainly use the library, if you'd like to follow me.'
Alexandra picked up a handbell. Its tinkle saw the green
kitchen baize door open. An aproned woman appeared.

'Martha, we'll have tea in the library,'

'Yes mam, and the Colonel will he be--?'

'Give him a call will you please Martha. I expect he's on
the lawn with the bees.'

'Right mam, I'll do that now.' We entered the library.
A high-ceilinged room with a wall book case from floor to
ceiling. Easy chairs were grouped around a black marble
fireplace.

'Do take a seat won't you James?' I chose to sit at one end
of a sofa.

'There he is.' She was by the window. I got up to look.
Colonel Stewart had removed a netted bee guard. Martha
undeterred by the bees was talking and at the same time she
pointed toward the library window.

'How many hives are there I asked?'

'Six. There on the small lawn James. They'll need to, be
moved to the kitchen garden. Perhaps James you could assist
Reginald after we've had tea. There's a spare bee guard. Not
allergic, are you?'

'No.'

You'll no doubt need to set the fete up in advance. That's
if our garden is suitable?'

'Oh yes, very much so,' I replied.

After we'd had tea, I assisted the Colonel to gently wheel
each hive on a boarded pram chassis from the small lawn

and across the main lawn up to the kitchen garden

'It's very good of you and Mrs Stewart to open up your garden like this.'

'Like to do our bit, you know.' We've outside facilities. Perhaps the men could use these and the women the staff kitchen toilet.'

'Yes, that would be fine, I said.

'We've no children Jim and Alexandra likes the social side, probably more than the sailing.'

'Every bit as important to have a thriving social membership, Colonel. Thank you very much for this opportunity to help raise funds for the club's new start platform.'

'Like to do our bit, you know. You'll need to set up. Can this be managed on the Friday before.'

'I'll make sure it can, Colonel. I'll make sure it can.'

'I met up with Julie at the Stewarts' on the Saturday of the Garden party.'

'You decided to come then?' I enquired. Trying to seem disinterested.

Alexandra wanted to know if I would assist James.'

'In what way,' I asked. Since I was the main organizer, this seemed an appropriate question.

'Assist you, James.'

'Alexandra didn't mention this. To do what?'

'We're to meet Dick West when he arrives shortly from the TV station. You are the social secretary.'

Right. And to do what?'

'Apparently they know one another.' We're to escort him to the front door so he can freshen up is how Alexandra put it. That's before the ribbon gets cut. He'll also need a ten-shilling note to spend on the stalls afterwards.

'Okay that seems reasonable. He'll probably have

attracted visitors to the garden party.

Day of Garden Fete

We were stood on the path above the main garden. A mixture of cigarette smoke and cheap perfume floated up from the stalls. Although the official opening was not until eleven most of the stalls were in action, with a queue formed around the Calor gas fired tea urns. It was ten thirty when I heard the Austin Shearline sweep up the drive way. Only cars and taxis, that dropped off passengers were allowed to the house's front driveway. It was Julie who said,

'That could be Dick West.' Her eyes lit up. Even minor celebrities can cause excitement. When we turned into the parking space in front of the house, Dick West whom I'd met at the yacht club stood alongside a chauffeur driven car, which presumably belonged to the television station

'Good morning,' I said. Good of you to come Dick.'

He walked towards us from the car

'Jim. Jim from the club isn't it.' He knew full well who I was.

'Yes. We're tasked as greeters.' Julie was all smiles when she said,

'Alexandra has said that you can freshen up in the house.'

'And the fete officially opens at eleven?'

Yes, I said, but you can cut the tape earlier if you like.' I looked at my watch which said ten thirty. It was Julie who pressed the doorbell of a front door held open with a black door stop in the shape of a yacht. Moments later the glass door midway between dimpled glass windows opened. Alexandra spotted Dick West immediately.

'So good of you to break off from your busy schedule to visit us Dick.'

'Not at all Alexie it's my pleasure.'

'Dick won't be long. You two are alright waiting?' This was more statement than question. I sat opposite Julie on hard-oak chairs either side of the red tiled porch. It was at this point when I think Julie's star struck feelings for Dick might have ended. Through dimpled glass windows Mrs Stewart and Dick West were seen to be clasped together as if love-starved before they disappeared from sight into the adjacent hall space.

Twenty minutes must have passed before they reappeared. Alexandra, her face flushed, opened the door.

'It's ten to eleven. You'll just be in time.' She said to Dick West, more than us.

Dick West cut a white tape, with garden shears and called out,

'I'm delighted to declare this Sail Garden fete open.'

The tape stretched across a trailer and acted as a presentation stage with a beach sea painting by Marcia. Propped up for a background. Dick was accompanied around the Garden Party stalls by Julie and myself. At twelve, his car returned and he was whisked back to the television studios, presumably.

A cloudy start encouraged visitors who would most likely have visited the beach, otherwise on a sunny day. Mid-afternoon the sun broke through. I was inside Marcia's conical tent having my palms read.

Apparently, romance was on the horizon and it involved the yacht club, but I needed to up my game she said. No one specifically mentioned though. Marcia moved on to financial matters. I only heard the words

'A promotion might be due for you,' when a woman shrieked. Flinging open the tent flap I went outside. She ran across the main lawn pulling at her hair. Others smacking arms and legs. Colonel Stewart appeared with a smoke diffuser. Bees had swarmed Two separate trails of buzzing queen bee followers weaved across the lawn and made for the branches of trees at the far end of the garden, but intermingled with people on their way. Perhaps, it was the less ardent follower bees which attached themselves to the wisps of candy floss held by now screaming children. More distressing for women was bee hair entanglement. Hair spray maybe attracted the bees like sugar in the candy floss.

There was a rush up the steps from the garden. Mrs Stewart opened a large window which went into a main room. Within fifteen minutes there was nobody left in the garden. They'd all made their way indoors. It was like a casualty ward for bee stings.

I assisted Julie to dab with blue pads and Dettol those bitten. Moans and complaints lessened when Colonel Stewart offered sips of brandy to bee sting casualties. The bees brought the fete to an end. Fortunately, no one was dangerously allergic to bee stings.

Ian Hurst published an article in the Herald recommending the sail club's entrepreneurial skills employed to raise funds, in the sporting column. No mention made of two swarms of bees, which prematurely ended proceedings. His earlier damaging headline perhaps now forgiven by sail club members.

An English teacher who visited Buckfastleigh Abbey, recounted a strange apparitional event to author's school class in 1954. Gave idea for - Venue for A Delegation sixty-four years later.

Venue for a Delegation

Pink blossom, daubed an avenue of cherry trees, caught in still air; near silence save for a buzz of spring bees. This, yes, I remember this from that visit to Broadhurst Abbey. It all began with that good feeling of being alive to nature's resplendent new life. I later promised Brother Patrick not to divulge my experiences at the Abbey, but when the Abbot message said that he'd passed away, I decided to write an account of this visit in the spring of 2004. I can only imagine that you're reading or listening to this, because I listed it among "unexplained phenomena," but wanted to remain true to Brother Patrick's request whilst alive. Yes, even this account of my visit to the abbey released by someone's delve into documents, projects, my voice in a somewhat ghostly manner! This is a faithful account of what occurred. My hope's that it's understood my promise to Patrick was not broken explicitly by me, at least whilst alive. After, this introductory note there should follow an account recorded of my then visit to the abbey, which I wrote a week after Brother Patrick's death and stored as explained under "unexplained phenomena."

A visit to Broadhurst Abbey – Spring 2004.

My employer, "Brandon's Wines for the connoisseur," booked the Abbey's delegation hall on later occasions, but this was the first. Monks at the Abbey, had developed a thriving tonic wine business across several centuries. Angus Cameron, Brandon's chairman, negotiated contracts to purchase wines and it made sense, to take advantage of a twenty per cent discount, should the company need to arrange conferences. Latterly, I was no longer responsible for this conference organization, once promoted to marketing manager for Asian exports. An account more as a memoir of an extraordinary event, than to record the reason behind my visit.

It was later on, but in accord with a previous determination of mine that worship of good and evil can exist side by side. I recalled a terraced house next to a Cathedral, where occult practice took place. I declined an invitation, at the time to attend a meeting, because I considered dark forces might well choose to camp next to this place of religious gathering. A demonic plan, might be in place, to hook stragglers away from a Cathedral's luminosity. But I'm ahead of myself. This encounter started after an email from aforementioned Brother Patrick.

A message, from the Abbey office began with Good Morning, blessings to you, Andrew. Nothing, really out of the ordinary. This, from a man dedicated to the Lord's service. In fact, quite refreshing from a plain good morning or, Hi or even Hi Andy. Our Company Secretary had pre-booked my visit for three o'clock that Friday. "If this is unsuitable please feel free to suggest another day," were Brother Patrick's words. No, that sounded good. End of week and perhaps I might be able to sample some of their famous Abbey wine. He went on to message that I should be sure to ask for him by name i.e. Brother Patrick, because a booking for their hall could only be arranged through him. Attached was a brochure with venue photos and additional blurb. At the close of message Brother Patrick, again said that I must be sure to insist that I was there to meet with him. This seemed like a reasonable request and thought nothing more about it, as I remember.

I parked in the visitor's space, on arrival, climbed steps with railings festooned with white clematis, through double doors to the reception area. I expected at reception to meet with one or other of the brother monks but in the reception, cubicle was a young woman, who wore a dark navy suit and cream scarf which I noted was dotted with miniature pictures of the abbey. Apparently, admission spaces open to the public were monitored through a recruitment agency. Both hall and immediate area supervised and staffed by outside contractors.

I placed my lap top case on a chair by the reception desk, to search for my card. I realized that I'd caught the attention of the receptionist when she swivelled away from the screen to face me.

'Hello,' I said. I'm here to meet with Brother Patrick about the booking of the conference Hall.' She smiled back from where she was sat.

Hi, good morning welcome to Broadhurst.' And she got up and walked to the immediate desk area where I was standing.

'Can I be of assistance?' she enquired in a polite tone of voice.

'Andrew Parkin.' I placed a visiting card through the window space of the reception foyer.

'I represent Brandon's. That's Brandon's Wines for the connoisseur,' I continued.

'What an attractive conference venue you have here.'

'Yes, it's very restful away from the city. Andrew? Andrew Parkin.'

'Yes, that's me.' I repeated.

'That's fine. Brother Patrick said that he's expecting you. I'll just message him to let him know that you're here,' and she returned to the screen. A large entrance hall displayed illuminated maps of the front and interior of the conference hall. Also, pictures of underground cellars and large photos of what I assumed to be a vinery. Tonic wine making dated back centuries, but mainly imported grapes and other ingredients were employed. A warming of the climate recently enabled the abbey to grow its own grapes I'd read in the brochure attachment.

'Mr Parkin,' I turned to face the open widowed reception.

'Brother Patrick will be down shortly and has asked if you can wait in the refectory.'

-And where's…?' A hand held out directed my attention, as she said,

'Oh, that's through double doors across there.' Index finger – pointed to the far side. Self-evident once I noticed an illuminated sign.

'Yes, of course… and thanks, for your help. Oh, is there a Wi-fi connection? She reached below the desk top and produced a slip of paper and gave it to me.

'Thanks very much for your help, I said and walked across to push open one of the double doors. A waft of cooked food lingered from lunch flowed out but was dampened by coffee aroma.

A serving counter at one end with stacks of trays visible in front of a steel tracked shelf led along an outer edge of serving area to a cash point. Visitor groups, scattered, across the large tabled area in front were in animated conversation. No one else visible, apart from a man and woman behind the serving area. I decided to sit at a corner table to the right of the main table area. Had I expected to see monks in robes and cowls about the place? Yes, but this refectory was for visitors on an open day to the Abbey as well. I'd stopped at a service station for a coffee and decided to sit at a corner table. Admit, to being absorbed as I read a financial report of company progress on screen when a deep slowly spoken voice interrupted my concentration.

'You are here to reserve the hall. I can be of help?' I looked up and across to see who was addressing me. A monk was sat directly opposite. A hood or cowl allowed view of grey, blue eyes, furrowed forehead, nose and chin.

'Yes, that's right. You're Brother Patrick? I reached my hand out but back, when this visitor remained with fingers inter-locked on the table.

'Brother John. It's not necessary to talk with anyone else. I have access to all vaults of stored wine. Keeper of the keys to all parts of the Abbey,' he replied. Probably a mistake, now on reflection, but I decided to play along.

'You can show me around the conference hall then?' A group, at the front, got up and walked toward the exit.

'Yes, later, but the wine vaults are more interesting. Look,' parted fingers, enabled his right hand to reach down to lift a silver chain to reveal large keys on a key ring, which he held above the wooded tresle table, allowing them to drop, and noisly hit the table. Sinewy fingers sorted through the bunch of spread-eagled keys, before he selected one black and rusting, ancient key. He held it up and pointed to a door in the corner that I'd not noticed before.

'You can see the cellars and taste the wine before you visit the conference hall.'

It was at this point that I stated Brother Patrick's instructions that I should first meet with him.

'I have instructions to meet with Brother Patrick.'

'That can happen later.' My iPad lit up and a picture

appeared which was worrying. It showed a wooden case of wine stacked across a wall. A stream ran mid-floor in what looked like a cellar. What was more worrying was the fade of light in the room immediately? around our table.

'You have a picture on your screen.'

'Yes.'

'Come with me and I will take you there.' The monk who named himself Brother John was now on his feet.

'This way,' he said and I found myself standing up. It was a decision that my body complied with seemingly no conscience decision on my part.

'Andrew. Andrew Parkin,' a voice called out from behind me. Already Brother John was walking toward the door his back toward me. I faintly heard a voice.

'Andrew. Andrew Parkin. Turn around and walk away.' I wasn't the one to turn, but it was Brother John whose life lit eyes changed for that of the dark orifices of a skull. A hideous apparition raised a fleshless hand. I heard a louder insistent command,

'Do as I say and turn around – now Andrew. Do this now, do this now.' I reached across, and noticed that my hands trembled as I grabbed case and iPad. Turned, and saw that brother Patrick, partly hidden in a swirl of mist was in front of me, arms outstretched.

'Do not look back. Do not look back.' he repeated. After about six paces the refectory appeared as I remembered on entry, where until his call had all but drifted away. As I neared, Brother Patrick lowered his arms and bowed slightly. I was never more grateful to be greeted by a hand shake.

'I apologise for keeping you waiting, Andrew.'

'Who they hell was that?' I exclaimed. 'I mean he said that he was Brother John.'

'Yes, the resident ghost. There's no record of a brother

John, that we know of Andrew.

'But I saw a door?'

'Imaginary. Look, he waved a hand toward the far corner. 'There's only wooden panelling. You're not worried, are you? He dematerializes in a short space of time. You looked a bit taken aback. That's why I called you. I was worried that you hadn't stuck with my message to meet with me. But you have now, so it's alright.'

'Yes, I did say that it was you I wanted to see but?' Brother Patrick pointed to a table nearer to the serving area.

'Shall we sit over here. Can I get you a coffee?'

'Yes, yes please, but − I mean, look, I didn't seem able to stop myself following his instructions.

'That's new. He's our resident ghost, you might say, and usually just dematerializes. An Italian buyer who visited, like yourself, vowed never to come back. But it did turn out that he never was going to, because he died on the aircraft taking him back to Milan. We were told by the company that he had a history of heart trouble. Never, fully explained what happened when he saw the ghost. Only, that he was invited to view the cellars, which was strange. I've always made a point of insisting that anyone who wants to book our hall asks to see me. I can't see that there was any connection with his death. A ghost appearance is very infrequent. I might say Andrew, you were honoured by its presence. How do you like your coffee, Andrew?

'Black,' I said. Brother Patrick went to the refectory and picked up a tray. It amazed me, it has to be said, that he made light of what had just occurred.

On return we discussed the requirements for the delegation. Before we left, I promised not to mention my visitation from this brother John to anyone. His parting words were

'We suggest there might be a ghost. It's good for publicity in one way, Andrew, but in another way we do like to restrict publicity about details. When brothers all similarly attired are in the refectory one could be a ghost. You do understand Andrew?' I said yes, but went away convinced that I'd witnessed a manifestation of something sinister that inhabited the grounds and building of Broadhurst Abbey. I never returned and made an excuse not to be at that delegation or any other held at the abbey. I did not suffer a heart attack, but it was in 2004 that year my hair changed from pepper and salt to white.

Author walked over Dartmoor with his father and friends before he embarked on career as seafarer. One walk was to Cranmere Pool. Wellington boots were worn. Not ideal for a terrain of turf clumps and strewn granite rocks! Fathers, friends wore lace up boots. More suitably attired and equipped with map and compass. Together with Dartmoor walks and summers on a farm, author reflects that there was, in place, a plan to toughen author up for future work life as seafarer.

A walk to Cranmere Pool

It was a good switch, sultry, sea level, turgid, Torbay, to, rarefied moorland air. We'd parked off road, that's myself and two, dedicated moorland walkers; Tom Broderick and Joe Smithers. We'd met, at the Ten Tors Inn, on my arrival in Kingsteignton.

'Need proper all-round exercise, Doug – not forty minutes slamming a ball, inside a box.' That was Tom's description of squash. I discovered they'd never been to Cranmere, but had walker's equipment, which included map and compass.

"Bring a packed lunch. We'll aim to get there about that time,' were Joe's parting words.

Ambitiously, perhaps, I'd purchased a haversack to carry my lunch in, and felt the strap pull on my shoulder, as we strode into the heathered moorland, questioning this decision.

It was late morning, and mist rolled down from the horizon, after an hour's walk. When, I mentioned, decline in visibility, glances between Tom and Joe, were those of concern, but didn't alarm me.

Within minutes, I struggled to see my hand, held out in front. Peril, for escaped prisoners on Dartmoor, became apparent. An impossibility, to get off the Moor, in such conditions. Local people, were known to leave food outside their cottages, when alarm was raised about an escapee A ploy, to deter break ins.

We stooped, huddled, around a giant granite rock, dampened, with fog. Tom's torch managed to light; a Perspex protected map. A dog's howl, would've been all that was needed to terrify me. A drip, drip, of condensed fog, came from nearby gorse.

'This rock!' Tom slapped it with his hand – 'is marked. And here's the Pool.' He let the torch pick out, a dark spread, further north. Compass, needle gave a NNE course direction.

'I'll lead the way. We'll stop every fifteen minutes to estimate, position and direction,' he said.

'Sounds good to me.' I said, with zilch experience, of these conditions on land. Happy, to let these two make decisions. Fifteen-minute, stops to define position, resonated with shipboard, navigation checks, when coastwise.

'There's food in a covered bowl and blankets in the shed. There'll be a search party 'afore long. Better you to keep on the move.' A disembodied voice came from within the fog bank ahead.

'She thinks, we must be escaped prisoners,' said Tom. We walked closer. A fuzzy light, in an upstairs room, appeared.

'We're walkers on the Moor – not escaped prisoners,' called back Tom.

'I'd not be knowing, come closer.' We were already,

walking, toward, voice and building. Suddenly, I stumbled against a garden gate. A front porch, to a smallish cottage was visible. Light, flowed down the path.

'There's three of you then.' The woman's strident voice called out.

'Where be you to? Look too well fed, to be prisoners.'

'Kingsteinton.' We left Joe to do the talking.

'Walkers out of Kingsteinton.'

'Ah, not so bad as Exeter. We're safer out here though,'

'We didn't enquire further about what she meant. It could have been a comment on the weather. It was a bit weird, when she followed with,

'Them targets, churches and large buildings.' It seemed, a funny appreciation, of fog effect.

'You can have tea, to warm you. Jeff, my husband's asleep, in the front room.

We hadn't planned on a break. But it was welcome. We were soon, sat around, a scrubbed table.

'No sugar 'till next week, she said. 'Milk with your tea? She asked. 'Just made Jeff tea. A kettle, whistled atop an Aga. Kitchen primitiveness didn't strike me as unusual.

Thank, you Mrs -?' Joe, was interrupted.

'Joan Weston,' she said. We remarked on the welcome break. Accustomed, to abruptness, from country folk toward townies, her manner didn't faze me, as three mugs of tea were placed on the table.

'Have to leave you,' she said. Utilizing the tea tray, she lifted a latch to the front room, and called back – 'let yourselves out.'

We'd brought damp mist with us, but once outside, sun had eaten the fog, save where it still swirled around the cottage. As suddenly as it appeared, the blanket mist was gone.

We arrived at the Pool at about two, and sat in the heather to have lunch, before investigating the Post Box, which contained a letter, for us to take. Tom left a message. To canvas Government Authority, through his MP for additional, Dartmoor Preservation funds.

A week later I met up with Tom, at the Ten Tors, poring over a detailed moorland map, which featured The Cranmore Pool area.

'Come here, Doug,' He called out.

'Interesting, I said when I got close enough to see the map.'

'Yes, more than that,' he said, and pointed his finger at a building marked derelict.

'That's the exact spot where the old dragon invited us in for tea.'

'You sure?'

'Certain. And I've looked up its history. Their cottage received a direct hit from a Messerschmitt Br 109 bomber on its return from bombing Plymouth, in 1941.'

'You mean, there's no cottage there – no one living there.'

'Have you ever heard of time portals, Doug?

Unsettled by the claustrophobic atmosphere of large city centre stores author resigned from a management role with BHs in 1975 and was offered temporary work at Market Harborough postal delivery office and remained, apart from time as a Postal Services Representative, for twenty-seven years at MH Royal Mail Office, with additional Christmas parcel sorting on nights at Leicester's Head Office.

Roles included postal driver on delivery and collection, with station work and main delivery and or road collection to and from Leicester City Head Office. Covered for cleaning staff when they were on leave.

Author, trained as a St John's Ambulance First Aider and also as a work place trainer for Royal Mail.

Postal deliveries completed by cycle and foot for remaining years. Near to retirement author was granted a transfer to Royal Mail Radstock office and then Royal Mail Frome Somerset. Town delivery walks were performed in both areas.

In retirement author returned to a retail management role, in assistance of eldest son with growth of nine retail outlets in the south west. At the time this retail store business was the largest purchaser of stationery for the region. It was in 2005 that writing in earnest began, which led to publication of a number of novels and anthologies. In 2016 a blog site was started.

Postal Christmas Preparations (Circa 1980) is a life recall at a dispatch and delivery office in a market town, by the author, who experienced many delivery Christmas's with Royal Mail, apart from those passed aboard ship at sea or in foreign port.

Postal Christmas Preparations (Circa 1980)

Parcels badly wrapped; cards with little or no address; damp patches that seep from bottles, smashed when poorly wrapped and poultry with a label around its neck. Before that melee from future time, Parque floor will be prepared with increased floor fittings. Optimization, of space, where more drop bags are hooked in place for letter bundle and packet dispatch to London districts, Scotland and overseas. A back room opened with sorting frames, for cards and letters, to cope with high volumes, which will need to be broken down into regions and counties before bundled into bags. Installation of another stamp cancelling machine to handle Christmas cards.

Now, **before** that cry of **"have you got the Christmas spirit, yet?"** And well away from another seasonal question – **"Are we at the peak yet?"** *(Followed by a management walk past, with an offer of Quality Street, from a family sized tin to frazzled post people, with some snaffling a few)* – **New rotas,** will need displaying, entitled **"Christmas Pressure."** 0430 start to 1400 finish.

A twenty-minute break, after delivery completion, which when exceeded, could lead to wage deduction. Two – night staff, allocated to sort inward letters, from 2000 to 0500 and at the start of Christmas Pressure, City office to supply lease hire vans. **Preparation is all.**

Students and temporary delivery staff recruited to deliver

on foot or by bike. A back room with sorting frames in position for temporary sorters. Mainly women to assist in breakdown of outward mail. Supervised by Postmen Higher Grade, who will make random checks! Temps knowledge of postal geography not as developed as experienced postal sorters. Time plates removed from post boxes two weeks in advance, and a dedicated van driver, then to circulate the town, to clear all post boxes several times each day. Individual, walk post people, by then, no longer required to carry keys to clear pillar boxes. Letter card volume increase representing three per cent of total yearly letter postings.

Historical village arrangements, into play, where certain sub post offices from sixty villages will supply a post person. A farmer, student or villager put forward by a sub postmaster or mistress. Where, during the year, a rural postman might deliver to maybe four or five villages, delivery pouches then, for that individual village, dropped, at allocated sub post office. Delivery time, still stretched, for the rural post person, once count-down begins toward Christmas Eve. Now well past, those times in 1878, when postal customers were requested to post early, on Christmas Eve, to ensure delivery!

Main business recipients of mail, in the town centre, will be listed and offered an opportunity to collect their own mail. Banks, building societies, travel agents and other premises.

Delays, inevitable with high volumes of Christmas post. Days soon to be identified in the count down to the final delivery day of Christmas Eve, with the outer labelling on dispatch bags for day 20, 19, 18 etc…

In the City, the Lord Mayor, finally shown around to see how mail has "all," been cleared. Perhaps only a rumour that delayed postal bags are stationed in a skip to sit, in a lift, between floors.

History of art was a unit of study in a university course, which author followed after sea service. Royal Mail, the organization were supportive of educational endeavour. Author attended cookery classes at a local college. Teacher was employed at HMP Gartree to prepare prisoners for their life at the end of sentence.

Other courses sponsored by Royal Mail, which author completed included Advanced Level Mathematics, Psychology, Theatre Studies and computer studies. Author has attended two computer studies courses, each of which led to a regressive influence on computer skills! Hopefully tutors in 21ˢᵗ Century have a better understanding of the subject and how to teach it?

A former naval officer, with seafaring background like the author ran a course on communications skills, which encompassed behavioural patterns – of submissiveness, assertiveness and aggression, which relate to a work place environment, but also in everyday situation. Author would recommend this course profile to British managers throughout the UK.

A Renaissance Painting

An early wall fresco which "speaks to the viewer," but with issues over materials, passage of time, and attempts at restoration, has left a fresco of *The Last Supper* by Leonardo, in a poor state. That first wow factor of presentation taken away. Latest restoration work was in 1990. Leonardo's study concentrated on the moment when Jesus sits down with his disciples and declares,

"Verily, I say unto you that one of you shall betray me." (Matt. 26.21)

There's a *Copy** *after Leonardo's Last Supper,* oil on canvas, by an unknown 16th Century artist, which displays detail no longer available in Leonardo's wall painting. That Leonardo, at an early age, was a master of colour and presentation, not doubted. In the *Baptism of Christ,* of which the main work was by Andrea del Verrocchio, Leonardo painted an angel, who holds Christ's garments, with eyes directed toward John about to baptise Jesus. The two figures of angels, painted by young Leonardo, at possibly aged15, considered to be of a higher standard than that by Andrea. A reason why Andrea never touched colours again. He was so ashamed that a boy understood their use better than he did, apparently?

Although, *Copy** of the last supper, has freshness of colour, it is unlikely to portray that vibrancy, which would have burst from Leonardo's freshly commissioned work, Circa 1495 – 1498.

That Leonardo was both artist and scientist meant

that particularly, in this work, precision of placement and perspective, entrances the eye to focus on the triangulation of Christ beneath a centre lit back panel. Emphatic portrayal of three panels, together with that of three right and left wall pillars. A work of symmetry, that could be said, to be disturbed by four cluster groups of disciples either side of Christ, in disarray at announcement by him that one of them would betray him.

Portrayed seated or standing, Leonardo captures disciple's role and identity for the viewer of particular disciples, gathered either side of Christ. This painted fresco, a pictorial role depiction, which spoke to those who were familiar with New Testament personalities, in the 15th Century, as today. There are various paradoxes. One of which is an over large table for the room, yet probably not suitable for sitting thirteen men or if certain modern conjecture would have us believe, also Mary Magdalene.

A simply constructed layout made, complex by Leonardo's perception, that

"Postures, gestures and expression should manifest the 'notions of the mind.' That each one of the 12 disciples react in a manner, that Leonardo considered fit for that man's personality. This gives complex varied human emotion, within a deceptively simple composition. Commissioned by Duke Ludovicio Sforza for the refectory of Santa Maria delle Grazia in Milan, Leonardo used an oil/tempera mix and applied it to a dry wall. Nuns and monks frequently sit for their meals with a copy of the Last Supper on their refectory wall. Leonardo's Last Supper portrayal considered to be one, if not the world's, greatest work of art.

Finely, calculated portrayal of gesture and facial expression, shown to have been captured with preliminary sketches. Face sketch preparation of the disciples Judas (180 x 150 mm) in red chalk and Peter (190x149mm) in black chalk, both at Windsor Castle, give credence to modern reports that he practised to achieve maximum variety in the heads of the disciples. A search made in Milan, and surrounding districts for strongly expressive faces, that could be used to depict each disciple. A belief, for Leonardo, that the character of a person was strongly etched in their face. Expressive hand positioning distributes across the four groups, a disturbed feeling, and incredulity that anyone could be guilty of betrayal, save for Judas's with money pouch on display for the viewer to see, together with display of a knife, which pre-alerts Peter's actions.

This cast of disciples, with their attitude, pose and relevance for viewers in the fifteenth century and today with prior knowledge of the gospel story. A need to talk pictorially to those who visited the refectory, many of who would have likely been illiterate, but who were nevertheless versed in the gospel story. The given character definition and instrumental role for these disciples, around Jesus can be seen immediately. Those expressed feelings of horror and disbelief, which emanate across the table length, at that moment, from Jesus's announcement. Yet, leave Judas exposed as the betrayer.

A stage like setting constructed according to the rules of central perspective. Lines of perspective meet in Christ's eye, to emphasis his central position. Judas holds a money pouch, whereas John does not know the traitor's identity. Jesus highlighted in the framed central window, that looks upon a rolling landscape.

Rules of central perspective give dimension beyond that for simplistic scene portraiture. The wall fresco captures the moment where Jesus speaks of betrayal. Facial, stance, character depiction and multiple hand gesture from the disciples, directs concentration toward the prime figure in the midst of the supper gathering. That the disciples are figuratively dressed in appearance and actions to depict their own gospel background. Separately, in the case of Judas's betrayal and in Peter, anger.

This portrayal of the disciples by Leonardo separates them into groups, and also seeks to tell their story role. Further desperate emphasis on how alone and isolated Jesus has become. The disciples no different from ourselves today when we have regard for others to see us in a good light. Driven by our own self-interest, neglectful of another's distress. This timeless portrayal of human kind.

An observed view of this fresco when displayed, for example, on a wall by slide show, tricks the eye, due to perspective which takes your eyes away from two-dimension portrayal into that of a three-dimensional understanding. You become one with the scene and made to believe that you are sat inside the room with the gathering of disciples with Jesus, immediately in front. The pillars move from the painting to either side and you effectively become an observer inside the room, at the time, and place of the event. This effect, together with carefully researched and considered composition, plus eminent artistry, gives this *Last Supper by Leonardo de Vinci*, a primacy of achievement recognized to this day.

Description: The Last Supper. Renaissance painting: Circa 1495 – 8. Leonardo de Vinci.

A fictional story developed from an event of this nature recalled by author's eldest son, while in attendance at a comprehensive school. Perhaps needs to be stated, that eldest son was not the perpetrator!

Dingley Park School receives assistance from Foreign Office.

John Burnham, Head Teacher stipulated that his door was always open to new students, should they need to ask "anything," about their school, on first arrival. Not strictly true, since after lunch and a couple of nips of whisky, he was not in his office, but busily roaming corridors and empty classroom/office, to switch off lights and appliances, not in use. A tight budget, meant no wastage could be allowed. A Head teacher, you might say, unwittingly, ahead of international awareness in need, to save the environment.

Teachers, believed that he was spying on them, from the corridors, but this was not the case. They were, however, diligent in not letting pupils out of class, unless absolutely necessary, in case they met up with Head Teacher Burnham, which could lead to a classroom visit or tell-tale story hatched, about them to the Head.

Wayne Scot, was sat at the back of Celia Stratton's Humanities Class, and made, as if to bite Bill Driscol's arm. A culmination, of several disturbances that afternoon. Celia, spotted rotund figure of Head Teacher, John Burnham, through the wire toughened glass window door and walked, in her stride across, to pick up Wayne's exercise book. She opened the door and turned toward Wayne.

'Come with me Wayne,' which elicited,

'Child snatcher.' from Dawn Brentwood, but was ignored by Celia.

'Mr Burnham,' Celia called out, 'Wayne's disturbing students, who are keen to study. I would like for my class's benefit, to isolate Wayne for thirty minutes, if possible, where he can complete an essay, due in.' She held up a blue exercise book, decorated with transformer stickers.' This sudden burst, into the corridor by Celia, with Wayne in tow, startled the Head, who sought, invisible presence when on light switch manoeuvres. He rifled through a cluster of keys and plunged one, into a vacant office door.

'Wayne can complete his essay in here, Miss Stratton.'

'And Wayne I will see your completed work before you leave today. Understood?'

'Yes Mr Burnham.' Wayne respected the Head, because his father, knew John Burnham from time in the Territorial Army together. Knew, he'd get it in the neck, if anything got back. This empty office, was due refurbishment. Polythene sheets covered furniture and the Head swept one, off a desk and beckoned Wayne over. A telephone remained on the office floor. Wayne, sat on the desk chair appointed, with exercise book and pen.

'Thank you, Mr Burnham,' said Celia, and returned to her class, with new found respect.

Significance of this interlude, in Celia Stratton's class was not apparent, until office manager Jane Tilbrook received, quarterly billing from British Telecom. There was an error, she believed, and photo copied the bill, to show all call listings. The one that must surely be an error, was for £80.000.15p.

'There's evidently an error Mr Burnham. No call could "possibly," have been made out of Dingley Park for eighty thousand pounds and fifteen pence.

'Leave it with me, Jane, I'll contact the billing department and see what's going on.' John Burnham, smiled with a confident smile, that Jane knew, might mean nothing further would be done. Where she would have to chase it up, with BT before a reminder arrived. In this instance, with budget restrictions heavily on his mind, John Burnham did call the Billing manager. He discovered, that a call had been made, to The Speaking Clock, over a period of not seconds or minutes, but months.

'No school can possibly meet this type of bill, which must be an error.'

'We can identify the phone for you, if you wish Head Master and you will need to contact the Home Office, for them to make an investigation,' was the reply from BT.

Later that day notification arrived, that the phone, in question was based in the office where Wayne had been relocated. He hurried to the Office, unlocked the door, and the phone was busily chanting "at the third stroke it will be eleven forty-seven and seven seconds etc…" The Head slammed the phone down and re – locked the door. He regained composure, whilst he walked along the corridor, before opening the school office door. Jane, breezily called out from behind her desk.

'Can I help you with something Mr Burnham?'

'Well yes Jane, I need to make a call to the Home Office.'

'That shouldn't be a problem. I'll get the Home Office on the line. Shall I put them through to your office, unless you'd like to make the call here?'

'No, no. I'm returning, now. Give me five minutes before you call.'

There was some relieve for the Head when he was told by the Home Office that they would contact BT and explain how a call was made inadvertently, through a phone being improperly replaced, in a now unused office. That a pupil had deliberately phoned the Speaking Clock and left the phone off the hook, was detail John Burnham, felt the need to conceal. But that the Home Office was involved and willing to look into the matter seemed like a positive step. It was later that afternoon when they called back.

'Hello. Am I speaking with John Burnham Head Teacher?'

'Yes, speaking.'

'It's Brian, from the Home Office. Hi. Regarding your billing for Speaking Clock usage with BT.'

'Hello Brian. Good of you to get back so soon,' answered the Head.

'Yes, well, we've chatted with BT and apparently the call went to Australia's Speaking Clock, which would explain the high charge for the call.'

'Really? John Burnham reduced his alarm response with a follow up of,

'Oh – and what does that mean?'

'Well, in a nut shell, Mr Burnham it means that the jurisdiction for adjudicating is outside the Home Office's orbit of involvement.'

'Who then can I contact to resolve the situation?'

'You'll need to contact the Foreign Office. Oh, I can give you their number – just a moment.' And that was how Head Teacher John Burnham at Dingley Park School, came to seek assistance for resolution of his predicament, regarding the school's billing, through the Foreign Office, for usage of Australia's Speaking Clock Service.

Rail journeys were inevitable for author as a merchant navy seafarer who lived in Devon. Main sea ports of Glasgow, Liverpool, Bristol Channel ports and the Port of London, necessitated a train journey either to sign on to board a vessel or at the end of an overseas voyage, for return home. On one occasion a ship was joined in Rotterdam. A fictional story written for a scary story competition.

Parthian Kinsman.

I boarded the train at Newton Abbot, bound for Liverpool Lime Street, with prospect of several changes on the journey. It was a good time to be exiting UK for warmer climes. An early morning departure of 0516 and expectation of few passengers, but this wasn't the case. A corridor train with four carriages, no doubt, others would be added on route. I choose a non-smoking carriage and struck lucky. Its first two compartments were nearly full, but the third with just one occupant, immediately inside. It was only after I'd sat by the window, removed yesterday's paper and placed, my grip in the net above, that I noticed a white duffle type bag and suitcase, above where my companion traveller was sitting. A bag, which reminded me of those photos of American sailors, who joined or left a ship with this type of bag, slung over their shoulders. My now companion passenger, looked up from his book when I glanced across and I said,

'Busy for the time of day.'

'I wouldn't know,' He replied, but this led into

conversation, because I said,

'Not a regular, on the train then?' Face, partly hidden by a book, which he closed. I'd sort of persuaded him into talking, but he didn't appear to mind. He lowered his book. Closer inspection, revealed sleek black hair, whitening at the sides, possibly mid-fifties, with a mid-eastern complexion.

'I've been visiting relatives, and leave has finished.'

'Leave, do you mean shore leave? I asked.

'Yes,' he half smiled. 'I'm about to re-join Parthian Kinsman in Liverpool.'

'Really, I'm in the same position. A Blue Circle Line ship. Mike Peters, Second Mate. In more formal situation there might have been a handshake.

'Jonas Faja. First Mate,' he replied. It wasn't that unusual to meet up with other seafarers, journeying from or to a ship. At least we were likely to talk to one another, where train travellers can shut themselves away, preferring to appear engrossed in a book, which my companion, might, who knows, have preferred. That's it when you meet a stranger on a train. Both can be trapped into a forced politeness. Although seafarers when they meet up can rival fishwives at their most talkative. My train companion's speech was though slow and deliberate and it seemed that he might have a prepared conversation. That he was First Mate did not create a seniority barrier.

'It's a journey I make regularly,' he said and then, 'We should have been given ammunition.'

'Ammunition?' I queried. He then corrected himself.

'Munitions, I meant munitions. We can be short.'

'Right, I said. We were amply provided for with ship's stores, but this was not always the case with some companies.

'Where are you trading.'

'To Cape Town, and you?' He asked.

'We're on the BA (Buenos Aires) run.' Rain slaked across the window, as the train left the station. I wasn't sure what to make of my companion. It appeared that he was preoccupied and only partly willing to join in conversation.

'In a few days we'll be away from all this.' I nodded toward the rivulets now running down the carriage window outside.

'Yes, that's true,' he replied. I remembered seeing Parthian Herdsman in Liverpool docks. A modern cargo liner and I assumed Parthian Kinsman would be similar in design.

'You'll have air-con aboard Parthian Kinsman? Makes life more tolerable in the tropics.' There was a nod of the head, almost like disbelief, and I felt that there was a distance of understanding between us.

'The buffet car is now open for coffee and refreshments, Ladies and Gentlemen.' I heard the adjacent door open and shut after the call was made. Then it was our turn.

Afterwards, I turned to my companion and said,

'Might not be another chance,' and got up.

'Will you be joining me,' I asked.

'I have no need, but do not let that stop you, please.' He said, and raised a hand, in confirmation, before opening and raising his book, to continue reading. I did have reservations about my choice of travelling companion, I admit, but when I returned the compartment was empty. My grip was still in the netting above, but there was no sign of the Parthian Kinsman's First Mate. Yes, it felt odd, but then he did appear engrossed in reading and perhaps he wanted to relish those last moments before being back at sea and only with seafarers.

It was mid-afternoon when I boarded M/V Albany Pride and the Chief Steward handed me my cabin key. We were due out of the pool just before high tide that evening. After the evening meal, Captain and pilot were in the wheelhouse. Having made final chart preparations, and while checking the radar I heard the pilot say,

'You'd be leaving now Captain, but we're awaiting on Parthian Clansman to clear.'

'That's a coincidence I travelled up with the First Mate, from the Parthian Kinsman, well part of the journey.' I happened to remark.

'That you did not Second Mate,' said the captain.

'That's right.' enjoined the pilot.

'Kinsman was attacked outside of Biscay on my recollection, Captain. Got out of convoy they say. Not a chance,' said the pilot.

'They'd fitted an after four-inch gun, but with no ammunition.'

It was known that merchant ships were given guns but no ammunition, at the time.

'They might have had a chance to hit back, but yes Kinsman went down with all hands.'

'You must have been mistaken. I know the First Mate's family, a Jonas Faja.

'There I can vouch for the fact that there's no way you could have met with the First Mate from Kinsman.

I didn't pursue this, but just said,

'I must have been mistaken.'

Bramble Cottage

Last Journal record, from Jonathan Pascal.
Trust account manager. August 2022.

Part of managing estates of bank customers, involved visits to deceased clients' house or cottage. Bramble Cottage, Buttercup Lane, was a third visit made that year, in 2022.

A sad situation since no living relative remained and it was the bank's responsibility to list contents and in particular, items of value, which before the premises were sold would go to auction. Penny Arkwright's will stated, half her estate should go to the Leeds Stray Cats Sanctuary and the other half to the RNLI.

Her brother, served in the merchant service and later died of heroin addiction, on the streets of Leeds and she considered that the RNLI, who fished him out of the North Sea earlier from a stricken coaster, were deserving of help.

Danny Bartholomew, a geography graduate from Leeds, was starting out in the world of trust banking and accompanied me to Bramble Cottage. My car was in for service so we caught a bus to Buttercup Lane. While aboard, double decker bus numbered 164, my mobile buzzed. It was supervisor, Steve.

'Need Danny back in the office,' he said. It was ten thirty.

'Jen Stuarts got a hospital appointment and there's no one to balance midday.' I resisted the opportunity to say "well can't you do it yourself?" A ping sounded, actioned by a woman with several carrier bags of shopping, and made me realize we were near to our stop.

'Okay Steve. We're nearly at Buttercup Lane. I'll get Danny to return to the office.'

It was out of order really, because two bank officials were supposed to enter a deceased clients' premises, with a premise that one would watch and verify the other while cataloguing items.

I turned to Danny, and explained the situation.

'Danny, Steve wants you back at the office, to balance midday. Jens got a hospital appointment'

Danny's response was a four-letter expletive, followed by Steve's name. Danny continued.

'Bet Steve knew about that. How'd he become head of department Jonathan?' I wasn't going to diss Steve, but neither did I call off the visit as I perhaps should have.'

'These things happen Danny. You've had an hour or so out of the office and it's all very routine. I expect Penny Arkwright's cottage will be full of old tat, and it'll be a house clearance job.'

I left Danny at the bus stop on the opposite side of the road and walked down past neat hedgerows, aware of the cottage's position from a previous visit with documents, which needed to be signed.

Bramble Cottage, empty for a number of months, I recall, showed evidence of neglect with dandelion leaves, which flourished through path flagstones. Straggling rose tendrils, wavered in the breeze giving visible expression to the cottage's name. Lack of garden attention, inviting nature to take over.

Bramble Cottage, stood apart, in the lane, from previous bricked bungalows, with concrete and brick weaved driveways, plus container plants to lower maintenance. I almost lifted the black hand knocker to strike the door. There was sense of habitation.

A Yale lock was fitted into the arched wooden doorway with a waist level keyhole blocked out. Maybe, a modification, to assist Penny Arkwright, with door opening in later years? On entry you walked through a small hall way with an oak chair on either side. A range of black wrought iron coat hooks held a blue duffle coat and green raincoat. Shoes, were neatly placed by row, in a shoe rack below, next to a short pair of green wellington boots. Miss Arkwright, on a previous visit, stood, in those very boots, deadheading roses with secateurs. Unexpectedly, I recall, she said,

'You'll be married, Mr Pascal or perhaps – once bitten twice shy?' Secateurs snipped a shrivelled rose. I didn't see how she could have known either way, but I said,

'I'm not married.' But was unwilling to volunteer further information. Certainly not that a girl I was in love with two timed me with her boss! Everybody else seemed to be aware, save me, which is apparently not that unusual. She continued, by saying,

'I was very much in love.' Why was she telling me this??

'But William died of a heart attack during a football match. I've never met any other man who how shall I say?

'Made the earth move for you?' I suggested.

'That's right. But a girl has to be asked, you know and I've never met anyone else, until…

'Until Miss Arkwright?'

'Oh, never mind, it's just the ramblings of an old woman,' and the conversation ended there.

On entering, Bramble Cottage, you immediately faced a red and blue patterned stair carpet. A door on the left, led to a front facing lounge, with another door at the end of a stairway. I noted the grandmother clock was stopped at ten to twelve. That insistent chime, which startled me last time, was not going to happen.

Curiosity, saw me walk along a carpet strip past the stairway toward the kitchen door. A kitchen which featured a table, but could hardly be called a kitchen diner. Appliances, consisted of an electric cooker, fridge freezer and washing machine. On the left wall was a landscape photo of Frankie Dettori, at the Epsom Derby, with Anaparnes. I read this from the caption along the bottom and remembered a cheque for twenty thousand pounds which went into her investment account. It was mentioned, in a letter, that it was all "thanks to Frankie." The photo looked like validation of the win made. Penny Arkwright mentioned that she liked to bet big on her favourites. I was tempted to ask for racing tips, but this would cross professional lines with my role as account trust manager. I made a note of the make of the appliances, suitable for auction, along with the grandmother clock, in the hall. All items, red stickered, to note selection. Auctioneers were given discretion and would leave items they considered inappropriate, in terms of fee and costs.

Everything, was neat and tidy and I knew that a home help from the village assisted Penny Arkwright for several years, until her death eight months previously. There was a musty unlived in smell about the place, which reminded me of early summer lets, left empty during winter months. They too might give off a similar "aroma," when you first arrived to stay, in the summer.

An inventory was taken, by me, of furniture in the lounge and dining room. Instructions were given in the will for an original home help, and finally carer, to dispose of personal items of clothing and to leave furniture and other possessions.

A relationship was built up in later years between the two of them, that's Penny and her former home help. It was stipulated, the carer, in Penny's final years, more than just home help, could have possession of any ornaments, books or non − jewellery items. A safe bank deposit box held jewellery and other items of value, collected over years, which the bank, in its role as trustee would sell. Little of great value left in the house, but everything I considered to be of saleable value, was marked with a red sticker. It was probably no more than half an hours' work. These visits were not that infrequent where long standing clients died with no living relatives.

With completion of red stickering downstairs, I began a stair climb to the landing. A scene of ducks flying across a pond with bull rushes, repeated itself and covered both stairs and landing. Plain cream background now faded.

It is, or was, at that point, I should stress, one of those situations hard to describe to those whose life experience has not encompassed a sense of presence? Nearest approximation that I can recall is that of an experience of consuming a fair amount of champagne, on an empty stomach. The mind can be altered to believe there's a presence, when partially intoxicated. A disturbing experience, since no other person is present.

I stood on that landing at Bramble cottage, with a similar feeling, without consumption of champagne or any alcohol, for that matter. Both, bathroom and smaller bedroom doors were open. A single bed, window table and chair and two small easy chairs, in the smaller bedroom were given red stickers before I glanced into the bathroom, which was empty, save for a bath, wash basin and toilet. Essentials left for saleability.

I walked toward the main bedroom and took hold of its door handle. Terrifyingly, a force took away the handle from my grasp and fully opened the door. I recall a shiver, which spread up my arm and into my spine when the door's handle moved out of my grip. A swirling mist confronted me and began to clear.

'Hello Jonathan I'm glad it's you.' I recognized Penny Arkwright's voice, but not a frail wavering intonation that I remembered from my previous visit. Appearance, was a younger version or so it seemed. There was no bed, in view, but I considered it was the lounge transposed to the bedroom.

'What's happening? I mean....'

'It's alright Jonathan.' This life affirming representation of Penny Arkwright, replied, while a vision, if that's what it was, emerged of a man dressed in dark naval uniform, who appeared near to where she sat. A small dog trotted into view to one side and sat at her feet.

'You've not met Rod, my younger brother?' The man's smile displayed family resemblance.

'It's strange,' she continued, 'but it was Marmaduke who came to meet me.' A vigorous tail wag followed when, what was surely a ghostly representation of Penny Arkwright reached to stroke this manifestation of Marmaduke. A cross between a pug and terrier. I was in a half state of wondering whether all this was hallucination on my part, but the presence thrust before me, spoke once more.

'I decided to return when a flow of earthly deliberation arrived. It was revealed that you were to visit my cottage, Jonathan. I wanted to meet you as my young self and yes, here my feelings are as strong for you, but we are parted. Nevertheless, I can wait with people I know and invisible visits are allowed to earthly time. You Jonathan, I felt understood and cared, and a visit might reassure that "all is well." No one is likely to believe that you received this visit, are they? You can see Rod is with me, as is Marmaduke.' I presumed Rod to be the merchant service young brother, who died from heroin addiction. This seated figure purporting to be Penny Arkwright, raised and turned her left hand toward the apparition of Rod, who I felt to be farther away, but aware, since a hand also reached toward his other world sister.

'It is strange do you not think? that it was Marmaduke who first greeted me and his spirit strength has power to bring me back as my younger self,' A reasonably sharp focus of tabloid vision began to fade at this point.

"All is well," she said once again, smiled and waved, before she vanished, to leave a previously expected view of the main bedroom. That was it! But it was close to real, as anything you might come across in your waking hours.

The bedroom was in view again with its easy chair, bed, cabinet and a single draw desk beneath the window. I summoned up courage and went in. Out of curiosity, I walked over and opened the desk drawer.

A slightly larger than A4, unfaded black and white photo, lay inside. It was a photo which was identical to the vision of Penny Arkwright, Rod and dog, I'd just witnessed. I picked it up from the drawer and held it beneath the window's light. Yes, it was most likely this room after all, but without the bed, because an identical window could be seen in the background. A photo may have been taken before the bed was moved in or had unseen forces kind of photo shopped it for me to find. I arrived at this possibility later.

I placed this photo, which was unfaded, into my brief case. This much I'm sure of.

It would have been of no value to an auctioneer or really anyone, was my consideration. And felt that Penny Arkwright perhaps left it there for me to find?

On my return to the office Steven insisted that he hadn't phoned me and why had Danny returned? Danny wasn't present, but did say, later on the following day, that "the silly old goat forgot he phoned you Jonathan." To which I replied,

'Really?' And left it at that. A mirror shiver ran through my body as when confronted by the apparitional figure montage that seemed alive. If it wasn't Steve that phoned? Who or what was it?

I do remember, looking forward to another look at the photo from Bramble Cottage, that evening, on return from the cottage. But it was no longer in the brief case?

Perhaps it was created from the nineteen-nineties, for my benefit, and returned to its particular time frame? All in all, evidence that would have made my account believable somehow erased. Record, of these events has been entered into my journal as witnessed, on that late July day, in 2022.

Jonathan Pascal.

"Nyama"

A twenty-nine, foot sloop; Bermudian rig with a fifty-foot mast. Cabined with two spacious bunks in main cabin, plus a collapsible poled hammock style bunk in the fo'c'sl'e. Originally, an open boat, with gaff rig, when built in Mevagisey, Cornwall in the nineteen twenties. White painted, canvas covered cabin, later replaced with Trakmark. Pitched pine decks ran around raised cabin housing, up to a three-foot bow-sprite. Nyama's previous owner commissioned new port hole rim strip covers. When priced for chrome fitted ones, opted to have the template hardboard dummy-ones fitted. Painted these with silver paint, which deceived a beholders eye unless up close.

A spacious mahogany boarded cockpit could comfortably sit six persons. Light ballasting meant that excessive red anti-fouling was visible when Nyama was at a mooring up from water's edge, to a gloss white hull. Possibly a none yachtie, would miss this seeming incongruity. A few oar strokes and Nyama's pram dinghy would have crew, helmsman and passengers alongside. Nimblest, in bow of dinghy, tasked with arm purchase and leg spring aboard, to cleat the painter (dinghy tow rope) before removal, of a short board ladder, housed beneath the cockpit seats. Ladder, then, was hooked across yacht's varnished mahogany rail, which circled a caulked pitch pine deck, for others to board.

Proximity, to harbour shoreside, meant afternoon tea or maybe, even cocktails served in the cockpit, would allow passers – by, a good view of event. Previous owner, it is surmised, was more into hospitality within the harbour bounds. Nyama, staying moored, rather than taken under full sail into Torbay and surrounding coastline.

A six horse power Stewart Turner auxiliary engine was fitted, beneath the cockpit's deck. Removal of short interior steps within the cabin was needed, when battery became flat, usually due to lack of engine use. A toggled cord needed to be wound around engine's flywheel. Cord yanked with quick release, to avoid finger, hand injury or worse, broken wrist. It might decide to kick into life after a few goes or not. Where "not," was the result, removal and clean of spark plugs usually did the trick. It would have been judicious to run the motor on every occasion when yacht was boarded. In force four wind and, above, sea spray or wave could drench the cockpit deck and seep down on to this marine engine, which, would have been better protected, within a housing.

Author's father was, at that time, a racing dinghy enthusiast. After race days his Redwing dinghy could be seen tied to the stern of Nyama. Nyama, was raced in handicapped events, and competed with ocean racers, Folk boats, cruising yachts, which included more pedestrian gaff rigged old timers. Father's friend from earlier days assisted with maintenance and was rewarded, you could say, by having use of Nyama to sail across to Elderberry cove with his family. They line fished with spinners to catch mackerel, and holidayed aboard on occasion.

Author, aged twelve, enjoyed rowing the pram dinghy as much as being aboard Nyama. In the autumn months, Nyama was floated into a cradle at high tide, situated at the end of a slipway. The two slipways adjacent to one another were originally constructed for naval operations during World War Two. Wooden legs attached midways either side plus additional props beneath the belly of the yacht supported this shore bound yacht, once parked for the winter months. Barnacles and weed needed removal from the keel and lower half before it all dried and stuck. Restoration of varnish work, repaint of hull, re-tar pitch of decking, was needed before re-launch in the spring. Memories are of sanding varnish work and applying anti-fouling to keel area. One year, pig iron ballast, was removed from bilges, wire brushed and re-painted. The fifty-foot mast, stored in a loft, needed a wet sandpapering before several coats of varnish. Author, assisted with yacht and race dinghy preparation, A mantra given, at the time, was that "two hours sanding equated to a day's sailing in the summer."

First visit to the river Fal

A Redwing racing dinghy championship held at Falmouth led to Nyama's coastal cruise from Torbay to the River Fal. That overnight sail to Falmouth was author's first view of phosphorescence sparkle in the wave break from Nyama's bow, which plunged forward at about four to five knots under mainsail and gib. Redwing Championships were a regular occurrence, in author's young life. Recall is of attending at Torquay, Paignton, Dartmouth, Tenby, Penzance, Weymouth, Falmouth. As crew member, in later ones.

With crew of one, agility, was required when the Redwing tacked against a head wind, with frequent going-abouts. A two-hundred-pound, knife like steel-drop keel was wound up, partially on a reach, and totally into the dinghy, with a run before the wind. Transfer of body weight aft required to help maintain plane position. The Redwing dinghy would then surf rapidly forward and overtake others, who were without wind and wave formation, to get themselves on to a plane. A brisk running/reach before the wind could create a skittish situation. Apart from a risk of inadvertently gybing, in a fresh wind, leaders could lose position where race dinghy followers were first to benefit from following wind. Their tactical manoeuvres, back and forth, earlier, against a head wind, to get ahead, maybe snatched away, on a run before the wind. However, a consistently well-judged head to wind zig-zag, likely to be main determinate as to who would win, with consistent wind speed direction.

Nyama's, passage to the River Fal from Torbay was uneventful, save for the novelty of sleeping aboard and a first taste of shared watch keeping for a twelve-year old. A week of dinghy racing followed. The Redwing dinghy having been towed by road to Cornwall.

A break mid-week, where another person crewed in place of the author, allowed time to explore the river Fal, while author rowed Nyama's pram dinghy upstream. A number of ribbed skeletons of boats could be seen on the river bank. The Fal appeared altogether a more interesting river to explore, than the river Teign.

Return from River Fal

Excitement, which translated to concern and worry in adult members aboard Nyama, occurred on the return journey. A force four wind developed into something stronger and the mainsail was reefed to half canvas with the auxiliary Stewart Turner engine running on standby. There did not appear to be risk in author's eyes, however crests of waves were whipped into spray and Nyama's rigging zinged in a way not experienced before. An ocean racer looked to be on a birthday treat as it romped past, in its element and with no reefed mainsail. A seasoned sailing companion of author's was quick to point out that these conditions suited the ocean racer, but we still had to make it to Berry Head, Brixham and conditions could worsen. A broken shroud could lead to a broken mast and the engine would have to fight a likely strong tidal flow; in any event should this happen. Redwing dinghy masts had been seen to snap, sometimes above the cross stays, in strong wind conditions Author's father, was persuaded to ease the mainsail and sail into the calmer Salcombe waters. Nyama, with permission presumably from marine authorities, was moored, and once sails were stowed and the green canvas cockpit cover in position, crew and helmsman went ashore in the pram dinghy. A Ford Zodiac taxi was large enough, with a front bench seat to accommodate, everyone from Nyama for the journey back to Torquay.

A footnote to the story is that father's friend saw the situation, that is Nyama moored in Salcombe, as an ideal opportunity for a family weeks holiday aboard the cruiser. Author and championship competitors who crewed Nyama enjoyed a rain free week, in Falmouth. Unluckily, as can be the situation in the south west, a week of summer rain, not unknown, to the disappointment of holiday makers. Heavy rain atop a canvas roofed cabin, caused leaks. Believe rain which lashed the deck also seeped through to those in the bunks. A sealant plug of affected areas did not stop leaks, but damp mixed with red filler, smudged on faces of bunk occupants.

Later, most likely from this incident, the carpentry and design skills of father's friend were brought into action with the stripping away of the canvas cabin top and replacement with Trakmark. A big improvement for those working sails on deck, with its dimpled non slip design texture.

Secret Cave

Halyards beat against the flag poles set out along the harbour wall. Shrouds caught by the wind made that tuneless chord that spelt of unsettled weather. The pram dinghy nearly got taken out of my hands when upturned. Rainwater previously captured exited – in a rush.

Tony was late, but since his dating of Katrina unreliability was expected. They were in love, as if that excused all recognition of others, who were not so engaged or trapped. I could see that this state might be seen as reasonable for winter months with Silver Spray stilted on dry land with no place to go. With existence no longer driven by that most important activity on the planet. Namely racing or sailing Silver Spray, whenever time allowed.

'Katrina would like to get to know you, Steve.' Tony said, earlier. The truth be known that one person could not manage the boat without some extra muscle. But I'd felt that his friendship with Katrina should be kept distant from his share in the boat. It was a four way share ownership. Tony, Peter, Karl and me. Outside of race times each was allowed a Sunday to take the boat out. You did need a crew member to let go of the mooring and handle the sails. On race days three people were required. We took it on a rota basis with each one of us dropping out once in the four weeks to keep the on-board weight down. Peter invariably helmed, simply because he was brilliant at it. Tony was joining me today to go to Blackberry cove. It was primarily to revisit a cave, which we found by chance on a previous weekend visit. We planned to leave after I finished work at midday.

'Oh, and by the way Katrina's joining us, Steve.' I was in a meeting with a group of managers when I intercepted my smart phones jingle.

'Is that a business call Steven?' My first name was called out by the area manager, in an attempt to grasp bogus friendship from a business associated relationship.

'No – Doug, caught me unawares – forgot to switch it off, that's all,' I replied. I promptly texted OK before cutting the phone – but was that it? No, it wasn't. Claire pointed a recriminatory finger, out of sight of Doug. Why did these meetings have to be so juvenile? Just then, on the slipway, my phone vibrated in my pocket. The furniture of the day's earlier event was still in my mind when I recognized Tony's number.

'Turn around Steve – "You've been framed."'

They were three stories up on the multi-storey, that's Katrina and Tony. He, in cut away jeans and tee shirt, phone in hand, leant over the rail. Katrina dressed in knotted blouse and wrap around mini-skirt. The dress statement looked more suitable for going to a pub than clambering about on a boat.

She smiled and waved with her right trainer placed on the lower rail with arm and hand around Tony. At least she wasn't wearing footwear that might damage the deck! Tony with cupped hands shouted down.

'Bit late – do you think it's OK to go out to the beach?'

'We can motor if it's too squally,' I called back. Faces, disappeared, while they walked down stairs to ground level.

'Don't look at me like that Tony I'm wearing a bikini

underneath,' she said when they appeared together on the slipway. Tony, who was dangerously smitten made conciliatory noises.

'That's fine Katra. I did say you just needed to wear trainers not shoes.'

'Nothing else? Are we skinny dipping then? Hi Steve,' she called out, waving in my direction.

'Hi Katrina, glad you could make it.

I never "ever" understood what Tony saw in Katrina – as a serious girl-friend. She was a picture to look at, yes. A model figure, which could have stepped out of a fashion swim wear shoot. Long curled eyelashes, chestnut hair, slim legs. You just knew the rose bud lips would pout enticingly at any camera.

The problem was that she had stepped out of the calendar. Beauty and desirability were attached to what was, a difficult and demanding personality. I wouldn't tell Tony that. I'd probably get a smack in the face if I did or the sharp end of his tongue. It was best to go with the flow, so to speak.

'The waters really cold further out,' I said. 'I doubt even whether you'll want to swim.'

'Not even a little skinny dip?' Katrina gave that look of a child denied a treat.

I unlocked the chain and cleared it from the oars and Tony released first one galvanized rowlock. While his right hand rested on the middle thwart, he flipped the far one up into position. I slid the blades in place and laid the oar handles well down into the boat. There was a wheel set into the keel, which made for an easy run down the slipway.

We both picked up the bow and walked it down, before releasing it a few feet from the water. It splashed noisily outwards, but I held the painter to pull it back to the slipway.

'You'd better sit in the stern Kat,' said Tony.

'What about my shoulder bag?' she asked.

'Give it here, Katrina,' I said. She pulled the strap over her head and handed it over for me to place under the middle thwart. Tony, held her hand as she boarded.

'Are there life jackets. I would feel safer wearing a life jacket?'

'They're on the boat, Kat,' replied Tony. 'You can put one on once we're aboard. It's not far to row. That's it there.' Tony pointed to our small yacht. A clinker built boat painted in cream with weathered varnished coach roof and cockpit. Only about two hundred yards from the shore. Tony assisted Katrina aboard. I followed and Tony pushed us away from the slipway. Once alongside Tony was first to board Silver Spray.

'You did say it's got an engine,' said Katrina as she held my shoulder and then grabbed Tony's hands to get aboard.

'Yep, but there's plenty of wind.'

'Tony, said, that I could steer once we get out of the harbour.'

'I said, "only" that I expected you could,' replied Tony. Katrina turned back towards me.

'You'll show me Steve, won't you? Tony's mean. He told me off for looking into shop windows when I was driving his car through town – I've never been in an accident, but he has.' Tony stayed silent.

We were together standing in the cockpit when she asked,

'Why is the cave secret, in the first place?' Made in an insistent, I want an answer way.

'Because we don't believe anyone else has discovered it before. There was something in the second cave, but the tide was rising.'

'And the torch battery was fading,' I said. 'I don't know Tony, that there was anything there, other than cave walls and the shadows that jumped behind the torchlight.

'Katra, Katra, a girl's voice came across the water from the slipway

'Prezzie,' Katrina called back and waved frantically.

'It's Priscilla.' A girl about the same age as Katrina, who I'd chronicled as twenty, but going on sixteen, in behaviour, was now standing on the slipway waving.

'Can I come? Can I come with you?

'No,' said Tony. Loud enough for her to hear. I called back.

'We won't be back 'til late afternoon.'

'I don't mind. Katra I've got the video on my phone from that gig at the Pirate and Fiddle.'

'You've got to let her join us, Tony then!' said Katrina, while she grabbed his arm.

'I'm not fetching her.' The shock of Tony not doing as Katrina asked perhaps caught me off balance. I received a plaintiff, winsome smile and like some prey mesmerised by a cobra I found myself uncoiling the prams painter from around its cleat. Pulled it alongside and jumped in the centre to avoid overturning it. There was less fuss from Priscilla, when she boarded, after the metal keel runner grated on the slip on my arrival. Once aboard Priscilla disappeared into the cabin with "Katra." Excited cries and giggles came out as they watched the video together.

'It's better Tony,' I said that it's not just Katrina with us.

'Why?'

'It just is.'

'And the secret cave isn't secret anymore.'

'Look Tony you brought Katrina along. I never asked you to. They'll probably not want to go inside when we get there, anyway. That's what I'm hoping.

Tony slipped the mooring after raising the jib. The breeze across the harbour was brisk enough to reach a little way along while Tony winched the mainsail up. I went about as we approached the harbour wall and we had a direct run across to the harbour mouth.

'Hey,' a cry came from the cabin. We were bouncing in the harbour mouth after a launch sped in before throttling down. Its bow wave disturbed the calm.

'You'd be better up here. You could get sea sick down there,' said Tony.

That was the last thing we wanted-sick all over the cabin. There was an easterly swell, which can lead to sea sickness.

'Katrina came out of the cabin first. They'd both taken their tee shirts off, which revealed bikini tops. Both tanned, but Priscilla more so.

'Can we sit up on the deck, asked Katrina?'

'No replied Tony, you'll fall overboard.' She made

a face to register disapproval. We'd brought the pram dinghy, which because of the following swell kept pushing forward. It almost hit the transom before it slipped back, with forward thrust of Silver Spray, a tow rope intermittently tugged the pram dinghy, aggressively. There was a heavy swell to start with, but it was a running reach all the way across to Blackberry Cove and a direct approach could be made. We left the threatening clouds behind

Priscilla said to Katrina – 'He's bossy.'

'No, he's just annoyed because you're here.'

'Are you annoyed with me Tony?' Priscilla was stood in the hatchway between cabin and deck. Katrina though engrossed with texting on her smart phone whilst sat opposite me on the adjacent bench.

'No. did Katrina say that?' Tony held the tiller behind him, in an attempt to cope with the inevitable yawing caused by the swell. Priscilla didn't reply, but just nodded back to Katrina, who returned to her main activity of texting. I felt fully justified in not having a female crew member aboard when racing, after dealings with Katrina. How could you be aboard a yacht and spend all your time texting? There was so much going on, like the taut snap and vibration across the mainsail as we caught successive blasts of wind. The flow of the yacht cutting through the sea and the view of the coast around us. How could you find time to text? I was waiting to meet a female of similar persuasion. I didn't feel that I held a misogynistic view.

The buffeting reduced as we went under the lee of the land.

'Thank goodness for that,' said Katrina, who'd finished texting and was taking more interest in what was going on around.

'Look,' called out Priscilla, the beach's empty.' A short stretch of beach could be seen beyond the white wave break.

'You can only reach it by sea,' said Tony. 'Those cliffs are sheer.'

'It's like a private beach, then. That's cool.' I chipped in with,

'There's a rising tide, we can anchor close in, with no fear of grounding later on.' Moments later the sail was rattling as we hove to and dropped anchor. Katrina dipped her hand in the sea, and shook her arm on removing it.

'That's cold. I'm not swimming in that,' she said.

'You don't have to,' said Tony. We'll go to the beach in the dinghy. The water will have warmed from the sun on the beach through the day.'

'All four of us?' Asked Priscilla. 'What about the boat?' She was more clued up than I'd thought.

'There's a spare anchor rope in the fo'c'sl'e, we're near enough to tie it to Sea Spray and run it ashore,' I said to Tony more than anyone else. The risk was that currents and the wind on the yacht might cause the anchor to drag. A line ashore was a safety precaution.

We went ashore with me rowing, Priscilla in the bow. Katrina and Tony fed out the line. It was quite heavy going because there was a cross wind. The bow crunched into the beach and Priscilla jumped out and with a cry of

'It's freezing here,' followed by sharp intakes of breath.

Katrina stayed aboard until we'd lifted the dinghy on to the beach.

'Your ladyship can disembark now,' said Priscilla. It was a sentiment that Tony and I might have shared, but was better left unspoken. Out of hearing

Tony said,

'Are we still going to show them the cave and the early grotto part.

'I don't see that we have a choice. It was the reason given for sailing over here and that was the bait you used to get Katrina to come with you. Anyway Tony we might not be able to manoeuvre that boulder at the back to get into the next cave.' I wouldn't mind if this was the case. There was a grotto type area with small stalactites and stalagmites in the cave at beach level. That might satisfy Katrina's curiosity.

'We could just say that it's a secret cave that reveals itself when the tide goes out,' I continued.

'Would you prefer to do that?'

'No, I want to have another look. We had to leave almost the moment we arrived last time, because of the tide.' We were interrupted by Katrina,

'Where's the secret then?'

'You mean what's the secret,' don't you said Priscilla.

'There's no one about. We could go skinny dipping,' said Katrina, once more.

'I'm not doing that. Stripping in front of them. How could you Katrina?

'I like the sense of freedom. We'd be all the same.' Priscilla wasn't convinced

'It might give them ideas that, you know, we're-'

'Available? Tony knows I'm not. Don't you?' Katrina raised her voice to ensure he heard, Evident that she wanted us to hear what was being said to Tony.

'Know what?'

'Know that I'm not that easy about getting my kit off.' Tony reddened. He was not really robust enough to stand up to Katrina, when she goaded him. It was also made clear who called the shots in their sex life-Katrina. I decided to shift the talk back to the secret cave

'Look, we made a discovery some weeks back. Over there.' I pointed to a dark opening in the rocks at the cliff base. It's covered once the tides in. It's known locally as the smugglers cave.

It'll be dark and creepy in side,' said Priscilla.

'I've brought two waterproof torches. We came out last time, because the torch battery gave out and the tide was rising. Tony, apparently hadn't that we'd found another grotto after diving into a pool in an adjoining cave. The cliff, beneath the pool went down about ten feet and then there was a gap, which separated the water on the other side. On surfacing I told Tony and he said,

'If, the waters not that deep this side it probably won't be the other side.' I didn't follow the supposed logic, but that didn't stop us getting under the ledge and surfacing in a much larger cave on the other side.

'It's not deep but you have to dive down and swim under the ledge at the bottom.'

'Really?' Said Katrina. 'And there's like a grotto on the other side. Now that sounds exciting. It's like all right to breathe once you get there?'

'Oh, yes, said Tony. You can feel a breeze like from above.

I was expecting a less enthusiastic response from Priscilla, but Katrina, said.

'You won't have any trouble will you Pressie. You used to dive for the school.'

'If it's cold damp and smelly what's the point?' she replied.

'It smells a bit of seaweed, and there's water running down the walls, but it's a cave and you can stand up and walk about inside,' said Tony. The clincher was perhaps the sudden squall of wind and rain that swept on to the beach and made us run toward the cave. The darkness needed some adjusting to, even with the torch light which danced across the ridged red cave wall when we entered.

'Look, there're small stalactites growing at the back,' called out Priscilla.'

'They're stalagmites,' said Tony.

'How can you tell the difference, anyhow?' said Priscilla. I was glad that Tony explained a way of remembering the difference.

'It's quite easy if you remember that stalactites come down. As in women's-

'Yes, you needn't explain Tony,' said Katrina. 'I don't wear them in the summer, so that won't be happening! She confided this with Priscilla more than with me and Tony.

'Does it end there? Asked Katrina, after she followed Tony's torch light across the inside.

'That's what we thought,' said Tony. He walked

towards a large boulder which appeared to obstruct any possibility of a path. It was Tony, this time who backed on to the boulder and raised his arms to extend across the boulder as I had before. There was no reason originally to do this other than to see if I could reach the sides of the boulder with both arms extended. I couldn't, but this action caused the boulder to pivot to the right and create an opening. The same effect occurred for Tony. The gap was wide enough for him to manoeuvre side-ways into the next cave where he shone the torch back.

'That's a fantastic discovery,' said Priscilla.

'Will it stay open? That's what worries me, said Katrina. 'Once we're inside can we get out?'

'It won't close,' I said until the tide enters from the beach.

'And how long will that be?'

'Two hours at least,' I said. The tides further down the beach this time. We've got longer. This appeared to satisfy Katrina but Priscilla said,

'That seems okay. Except there's no signal. Priscilla held her smart phone in one hand.

'No problem, I 've got a watch, I said. We can check on the time.' They looked one to the other and Katrina said,

'We can have a look.'

Katrina and Priscilla followed after Tony. Light from the torches showed the main pool, which stretched across from a slate platform. A smaller pool immediately ahead.

'It's quite warm,' said Katrina who'd removed a flip flop to test the water in the first pool.

'Yes,' I said that's what encouraged me to dive into it

after swimming across.'

'There was a panic when we reached the other side because the torch started to fade.'

'We never investigated any further,' said Tony.

'You, said there were shadows. Didn't you?' said Katrina.

'Shadows from the torch – until it faded,' I said. That seemed a reasonable assumption.

'These two waterproof torches have new batteries.' A sweep of the torch showed the caves limits. About twenty metres going back to the seaweed and barnacle encrusted back but no more than eight metres at the entrance. Constant tidal impact had layered the sides and hollowed out the back of the cave to more like ten metres. Sand was heaped there, and the cave' floor further back was smattered with rock pools.

'Shine the torch in front of us Tony, not on the back wall,' said Katrina. There was that green slimy weed on the rocks which led toward the main pool.

'It's slippery,' she called out. 'Oh my God!'

'If we walk forward four across and hold hands we should manage,' I said.

'We'll be alright if we hold each other's hands,' said Katrina, to Priscilla.

'You two just shine the torches on the path ahead!

'Do we need a piece of string in case we get lost?' asked Priscilla.

'Perhaps the Minotaur's waiting?' continued Katrina.

I heard their laughter echo back and forth now that I was further into the cave. It was, the intention for just the two of us to return. I admit I felt disappointment after the call to say that Tony was bringing Katrina. I'd sort of hoped that it would just be the two of us. A secret that would remain with us. There were prehistoric caves in the area. Perhaps if there were more stalactites and stalagmites and a few rock indentations and perhaps teeth of prehistoric animals, like the sabre-toothed tiger we could start a tourist attraction. I admit to the further development of this idea into a ferry charge to take visitors to the beach. A budding Disney theme park muse halted by a scream from Katrina. A rock crab disturbed by our presence fell to the floor of the cave with a clatter and scrambled away.

'It won't bite you,' said Tony. 'It's too small.'

'Look,' I said. These torch batteries don't have a long life. I'd like to dive down to the other side. I'll put the torch in the water and you three will each see it when you dive under the ledge.' After the shriek from the crab incident there was some doubt that Katrina would be prepared to dive into the water, but Priscilla was the courageous one.

'Katra, I'll dive down with Tony's torch and wait for you.'

'That's a great idea.' Before Tony could contribute either way Katrina grabbed the torch and handed it to Priscilla.

'Go on then Steve,' she said. I placed the torch on the cave floor and removed my tee shirt, as did Tony. The two girls their shorts.

'Okay,' I said. Count to sixty before you dive. Tony you can follow Katrina and Priscilla.'

I made a smooth entrance into the pool, which was just

below the surrounding platform of rock. I felt the rock wall with my left hand on the way down until my hand touched the cave floor. Momentum from the dive allowed me to manoeuvre underneath. Within seconds I surfaced on the other side. A thrust back and forth in the water enabled me to scramble up into the new cave. Complete darkness surrounded me as I leant forward and dipped the torch into the water. About thirty seconds must have passed before Katrina spluttered to the surface ahead of Priscilla; followed by Tony, whose torch lightened the cave and with my torch taken from the water I assisted each one from the water.

'It's quite warm in here, but it smells of fish and seaweed. Both girls' appearances had changed. Long hair now flattened from the water. They'd both managed to bring hair ties and after a shaking of heads wrapped the ties like pipe cleaners around the bedraggled tails of hair.

It was Tony's torch that caught the fish bones scattered on ledges around the cave. Large fish. I imagined that they might be the bones of pollock, cod or perhaps sea bass.

'Look at all those fish bones,' said Katrina. 'Do you think they died in here? Like got trapped.' I was standing near to a ledge which contained bones.

'They might have swum in on the tide and got caught, but there's no flesh remaining and they don't look that old,' I said.

'That means that something or someone's eaten them,' said Tony.

There was a shriek like that of a trapped animal that came from a tunnel on the far side.

'What the hell's that,' said Tony. The shriek ended with

a shrill, high note, but this seemed impossible. In fact, the idea that the cave was inhabited I'd never thought about. I shivered, involuntarily. Maybe the others experienced a shiver from fear spontaneously activated in primeval response.

Tony's torch light caught Priscilla's wide-eyed look.

'These fish bones' are they the remains of a meal.'

'It's impossible, said Tony. There can't be creatures here. I mean creatures that are not known about.'

'It was a trumpeted shriek that an elephant might make.

I realized afterwards that the shriek and shrill note was a call. We'd been detected by whatever was living in the tunnels set into the cliff face. By then I was reaching a possible conclusion. This creature or creatures' dependent on the rise and fall of the tide to fish in much the way humans had for thousands of years. Next to one stash of bones were the storks of seaweed. A diet quite capable of sustaining an animal adapted to such a diet. This jigsaw completed on reflection, but not at that time. I shined my torch across to the side behind the pool. There were three tunnels and the shriek could have come from anyone.

'Whatever, it is it's not some trapped sea bird. Not with a powerful call like that,' said Katrina.

'I'm scared, but curious, if that makes sense,' I said.

'You're allowed to be scared, but let's not get too curious, Steve,' said Tony. The pool separates us, but what if it can swim across. That makes me dead scared.'

We didn't have long to wait. The creature came out of the furthermost cave and was in the shadow of the torch light, until Tony shined his torch directly at it. The screamed shriek repeated when torch light met eyes that were set in a crocodile-like head. Small hands rather than paws at its sides, like a tyrannosaurus, but no more than ten feet high. Orange scales, with a black under belly. It stood supported by sturdy hind legs. A scraping sound was made by its long tail that swept sufficiently to be visible on each side of its main body. It related to that experience with cats when tail movement is related to anger before a fight. It was moving toward the pool, but stopped and gave another piercing shriek, when the light from my torch reached its eyes.

'It doesn't know light. It's confined to the dark. We're scaring it said Tony.'

'There came a sound more rumble than shriek from further in the tunnel.

'That could be daddy croc,' said Katrina. 'I want to get out of here! They might feed on fish, but want a change of diet.'

'What if they follow us into the water?' Asked Priscilla. Tony was also training his torch at the eyes of the beast, which became transfixed and mesmerised by the blast of light.

'Look. It's no more than three metres down to the ledge. They won't be able to get under. You three make a dive for it. I'll keep my torch trained on its eyes. This idea sounds heroic now, but sometimes first decisions are the best.

'Don't stay a second longer than us,' said Priscilla, who was the only one who shared concern.

'Go, then,' I said. The three dived in, whilst I noticed that the beast had now turned to meet its larger version, which was both taller and broader. Although some way from the pool this one went down on all fours and was making for the pool at speed. It was in attack mode and I followed the others into the pool. They had scrambled under the ledge, but when I reached the upper opening, I looked back and the scales of the monster shone like phosphorescence as it rapidly approached. I felt a rush of water as its snout snapped shut missing my leg by millimetres. I surfaced in the adjacent cave to see Priscilla's hand held out. I grabbed first her hand then the ledge to lever myself out.

'Where are Katrina and Tony?' I gasped.

'They're outside.'

'They didn't hang about.' I stood up and I could see the concerned look before she embraced me. Both of us like creatures from the sea dripping with water.

'That was very brave Steve,' she said, before she kissed my neck.

'Aren't you worried, that those creatures might come after us.'

'I don't think they can get under that narrow gap. Do you Steve?' She smiled and held my waist momentarily before drawing back.

It was probably at this point when Silver Spray as the priority for the summer probably fought for poll position. It seemed natural to hold hands as we walked out toward the bright light of the beach.

'They're like Plato's cave dwellers. They don't know light. Not even shadows. That is their world in there. I think we should keep the cave secret.'

'What about Katrina and Tony?'

'If they mention it to anyone, we can say that it's a made-up joke. No one's likely to believe what we've just experienced. When we say it's all a joke it's more likely than not to remain a secret Don't you think Steve?' I realized Priscilla was probably right, but that wasn't the reason we kissed passionately before we stepped out on to the beach.

Tray for our time

A tray is where people gather. Stacked in piles, at an entrance to a self-service restaurant. Does each one garner news from tables attended through its day? Streamed filed knowledge update one to other when re-stacked. Slipped information for another realm agency. Fantastical to presume, yet if information is stored in small chips why not other agencies from a world, able to access everyday earth activity?

Native tribes people never wanted photos taken of themselves for fear photo or film camera photo, took away their souls. Floral scene of cottage all innocent to behold but, maybe, holder of energy and memory from the plant, flower, tree, even cottage brick, adorned and captured, pictorially on that tray. Wherever, smallish items are assembled for ease of movement; a tray can be seen to display items. But so varied is a tray's location. Hotels, restaurants, jewellery shops, homes, bedrooms, aboard planes, trains and ships. A tray to gather oil spillage at a garage. A tray, helpmate never far from human tribe.

Memory recall, of night watch tray, on ship's chart room floor. Covered with squared teacloth. Main engine vibration made spoon clink in saucer, plate chink with cup.

A tray of seedlings, in glass house, soon to be pricked for transfer from capsule to pot. A tray at a children's party. Forty items revealed to party audience for memory recall. Before contents are hidden from view by dark cloth. Each child to write down as many items remembered. Elder children most likely to recall most.

Ubiquitous nature of a tray. Not to forget Cadbury's Milk Tray. Neatly displayed individual flavoured chocolates in pockets of cellophane tray. Trays, often decorative, not functional, but still identifiable. Those glass topped trays with butterfly displays. Iridescent wings, where light made vibrant colour dart back and forth. Author's, given, to jumble sale by his mother. Later explained that butterflies are unlucky?

Trays associate with every day. From hotel, restaurant, private room and hotel bedroom. Plastic, wooden, brass, in silver with silver handles and sides. Luxury devolvement from simple tray in supermarket restaurant.

Today, there is lap top and iPad. Are these not trays? Advanced materialized form of the simple tray? Knowledge obtained from informed discussion received and stored. World-wide tray upload. Now, a tray machine of one type or other orders our daily life. Smart phones, lap top trays have access to knowledge no longer a humble carrier for, knives, forks spoons and everyday need for living. A lap top, iPad, maybe of extra-terrestrial, invention?

Information made physical. Translated through a medium we understand and are familiar with – a tray. Aliens bemused? Unable to understood human online obsession to view "cats." Where Light and dark exist. Good information found alongside or behind murky portrait of man's darker nature. Exploitation of others unversed in the wiles of charlatans.

A modern world requires all to engage tray like machine for job application and domestic fuel, phone. Even energy supply. This onetime artefact, escaped bondage from simple form to become master in digital technology?

A Retail Chain Store

Name lettering was in embossed red and gold, before the sharp coloured glass panels and spread of plate glass which identified later stores. BHS Exeter, displayed the full name – British Home Stores. Managerial, say so, was that British Home Stores, spoke of the past and that the acronym BHS was now, the modern incarnation. On 15th February,1971 decimalisation came into law. Prices, to an extent rose, in a rounding up exercise. In those times, sales assistants were positioned inside two opposing counters. A quadrilateral shaped counter with front and back displays. The tills mechanical, save for an electric till, in the food department, which processed sales of, bread, cakes, biscuit and crisp. Counters belonged to departments. The fashion department, with dress rack displays, possessed, a free standing till unit. Cosmetics counters, front of store. were fitted with display units from Rimmel, Yardley and other brands. Hair spray cans warranted lengthy displays, and a woman's hat department, at front of store, featured on a right wall counter, where the left side front of store was given over to a food department.

A wedding guest might buy her dress from an upmarket department store, but would likely visit BHS for a matching hat. This very successful department in BHS stores evolved through the group taking on a hat buyer from M&S. Apparently, their buyer, was in dispute over some matter. She gave in her notice and was snapped up by BHS directors to front their millinery department. The problem for M&S was that the hat makers in Switzerland would only accept orders from the buyer whom they had built up a good relationship with. BHS benefitted not only from the acquisition of a top buyer, but also her list of quality suppliers, which gave customers a fabulous range of hats, to choose from. Young women were known to visit BHS dressed, in jeans and tee shirt, then with laughter try on hats, before a mirror, for a possible future ensemble or most likely for the fun of it.

Food and restaurants, arguably, took up a disproportionate amount of space in BHS relative to profitability. This did lead to ongoing modifications, whereby restaurants, at the back of stores could be taken out and replaced with clothes racking or counters. In every store a floor sales plan of both counters and racking was prepared weekly, by a departmental manager. Till cash sales for all departments obtained from the office for the just passed week, previous week and last year. Woman's Fashion, for example, which was performing well might show a 120% increase on the previous week and 220% on last year's sales. At the more sedate end of the business Household Goods. a 105% increase on last week and 118% on the previous year's sales. There were over fifty departments, and the store manager could appraise from a sales plan both good and poor performing departments. Seasonal variations saw ascendancy of floor space to woman's fashion in the summer, but always dominated best selling positions.

Both Food and Restaurant were labour intensive and commanded, arguably disproportionate space. Restaurants, in stores, with expansive table space and kitchens. A food department with back of store preparation rooms, could be seen to be costly where counter and rack merchandise would likely give a better return per foot of floor space. Exeter's Food Department's sales were strong, in that they could represent fifty per cent of a week's cash sales. A profit margin, though, nowhere near that of woman's fashion or other merchandise departments. Excessive shrinkage (out of date/or damaged food) – reduced in price. Maybe unsold, to be picked up for swill by a farmer, could soon reduce profits further.

Good product mix was a favourite term put out by company directors. Supermarkets can now be big on merchandise, but there have been failures, where customers did not take to clothes and household goods purchase from a supermarket chain. For BHS product mix, apart from a food department and restaurant, ranged across, lighting, women's fashion, handbags and gloves, men's, children's clothing, including back to school, shoes, toiletries, cosmetics, household goods/furnishings/curtains, watches, clocks leather goods, travel luggage, hats, toys – at Christmas – to name main departments. A restaurant at the back of the store, it was hoped would entice customers, and benefit overall floor sales. There will have been ongoing debate, by chain store retailers down the decades, as to the pros on cons of an in store restaurant. In some, instances restaurants have been ripped out and replaced with merchandise – similarly with store food operations. Presently M&S appear to have cracked the cycle of "shall we shan't we," with food by expanding their Simply Food Outlets. Fierce competition from major supermarkets back in the day made relatively small chain store food mix offering, vulnerable.

BHS Exeter store benefitted, at time of author's management retail training, in 1970, from having a skilled and customer intuitive food manager. Earlier appointed to area food manager, but then back in his former role. Stress of area food management led to abandonment of the role, with days spent parked in a car on Exmouth, sea front.

Now, at that time, back in a role which he knew well. Every morning a visit was made to the local market to ensure his Fyffes/Geest bananas were on front counter position at a penny less than that of the market. A crucial intermediary when for example a perfectly preserved beetle was discovered in the gelatine of a pie served to a customer in the restaurant. The beetle, an excellent specimen was cause of consternation to diner, but the food manager quickly responded by treating her to apples, bananas and oranges and a bag of wrapped BHS chocolate from his food department, which averted the situation from becoming a health and safety issue. After all, it was beyond the store's control, since the pies were provided by an external supplier. Having written that, one of the ways of maintaining supplier standards is for the buyer − to make visits to the production line and make sure that the food being bought for their stores is being prepared in hygienic and well monitored conditions. M&S, are known to be sticklers over quality control.

The Lighting Department at BHS could amount to thirty percent of sales in store. It was not only homeowners who visited to source table lamps, floor, wall and ceiling lights and fittings. In a larger store than Exeter, author was approached by a woman customer who asked if three hundred bedside wall fittings, in a particular bronze design could be supplied. They were, it turned out, for the new Holiday Inn hotel, near to build completion. The answer given was "yes," although the buying department were not best pleased, when they knew this cleared out supplies in the UK. Lighting sales, however, were up in store, that week. The general public when asked about BHS would quite often mention the Lighting section as being worth a visit.

Fibre glass lamp shades were popular, in this BHS Exeter store at the time and gave off a powerful oily aroma, in the back corner of the sales floor and also, where stored in the stock room. Another powerful aroma met with in the stock room was that of eight-pound polythene bagged chocolates sold in the sweets section. Cheddar cheese a quality cheese, when box stacked in quantity gave off a distinctive smell. Four thousand pounds, in money value sold weekly from a front end given over to Cheddar Cheese, in a store, for example. A good weekly sale, for the food department of that day, in the early nineteen-seventies.

Exeter store was an early store which was profitable at that time. Retail management training required that a trainee worked alongside a manager from each department. This included, merchandise, food, restaurant, stock room and office. The stock room had to handle the packaging and dispatching of customer orders. Curtains were a popular order together with luggage.

Part Two: Verse

All Thine

Grass in golden
glow.
Mud tide darkened stone.
River shows
coast in view.
Gulls, wheel, arc,
scream squawk,
swoop, strut,
snatch, grab.
All Thine.
Tide sneaks in;
slips on walkway
in transparent
squeegeed
flow.
All Thine.
White wave
foam froth
sprawls;
rock, pebble,
All thine.

Radiant daffodils,
dipped in gold.
Sheep, graze,
wind swept field.
All Thine.

School of silver fish,
weave in wave.
Sea floor creatures,
in protective shell.
Plankton bloom, feeds,
ocean giants,
that talk in deeps.
All Thine.
Rinse of rain,
clears air;
nature's wind force:
awesome, scary.
Sun's orb,
meets departs,
our waking day;
Adorns earth.
All Thine.

Smile of gratitude
from poor,
who've lost all.
Given food, shelter;
for these
are most loved
by thee.
All Thine.
Gleeful smile
of children,
who know they're loved.
Care for peoples,
in all lands;
beneath, gaze divine.
All Thine.

Earth, a school,
at times unruly;
brutal, uncaring;
where fights
over rights
to land,
spill blood,
in war.

Recognition, absolute;
This must be no more.
Unity of purpose.
Earth's religion
for all.
Primal call,
to save restore,
Planet earth.
All Thine.

It was
and is
always time;
to share, give replenish;
seek commonality,
where peaceful endeavour
refreshes peoples
in land respected,
sustained, nourished,
for insect, plant in
balance,
within a biosphere.
All Thine.

Thou gave
earthly dominion
to man, woman.
It is this time,
second, minute, day:
where conscious mind
of human kind
must adore, support,
life's cradle.
Be good to,
insect plant
and creature,
for earth is
garden of
breathed life,
delight and being.
All Thine.

Eternal Love: An Invitation.

Eternal love invites,
insists a presence;
more than just a glimpse.

An entrance made in
prairies of the mind;
to lift a heart.

Another's eyes
expressing care;
a voice beloved.

Words or music;
that caress retained;
and new memory.

Nature's voice;
that harmonizes;
but has ruthless strength.

Eternal, rhythm;
 – sunrise, morning;
evening, night.

To caress,
that inner being;
which feels, sees;
eternal love.

A Life's Journey.

Small, squalling,
needy, dependant,
seeking attention,
-meaning, reward.

Life maintained,
experience, gained.
Roles enforced,
developed, rejected?

Understanding;
we need still,
love for others.
Compassion, care.

Alone, sometimes,
but always part,
in weaving,
human thread.

We glimpse,
perhaps, startled
remind in everyday,
those who've left.

Seek in memory,
pictures, thoughts,
re-tell event;
their love and life.

Sometime;
somehow;
somewhere;
we also leave.

For people,
animals, sunlit
meadows, trees
sunrise and set.

On earth, where
hearts
sing, dance,
but also, sorrow.

A life lost here,
to be recovered,
anew within love's
perpetual grace

Light and Darkness

Light
gives colour
out of dark.

Light
takes seed
to plant.

Light
persuades
bud to open.

Dark
makes life
retreat

Dark
hides
from the light.

Dark
understands
not the light.

Spirit of Spring

It has to be the daffodils
which bravely sprout
from mother earth,
stung cold from
Arctic wind.
In shortened days,
of ice and snow.

How dare they dance
these ballerina's so
in delicate attire to
question winter's blast?

How foolish, perhaps
their belief, purpose, reason
to enthral our sight,
with rhapsodic dance?
When such a force,
that stripped the leaves
From mighty oak
inhabits still the cold dark earth.

Yet, perhaps their triumph
is more than just defiance.
Heralds of communication
beyond our eyes and ears,

dormant realms
good news of
return toward the flow of warmth and light.

A flower to greet,
applaud rebirth.
Vibrant early
colour in this forbidding world.
Primary brush strokes.
Scene setting for the approach
of Nature's master class.

Waves

Waves, seek,
to touch a troubled sky.
Give, roller coaster ride,
for those on
timbered bridge.

Bow sinks deep.
Rise and fall
makes fo'c'sl'e
bell to clang.

Shipwright skill
tested in
wave block flow.

Gentle waves,
trickle, tumble,
tease, dry sand.

Tidal march,
inland and back.
Seas, oceans, lakes,
wave patterns;
mood, expression,
occupies stream,
river, arterial spread,
across world hand.

Wind, tidal flow.
fearsome rise and fall
contrasts,
ray rippled,
golden sun dance,
'cross quiet scene.

In sunrise; sunset,
many a state,
water takes.

Waves visible,
in other worlds,
swirl human
voice;

music; picture;
verse; interpreted,
thro' worlds unknown.
Laced, weft in-air
hidden in flight,
to human eye.
Why would?
Molecules, atoms
decide to communicate
man's every thought and word
across barren spreads of air
and space?

Stream Reveals Secret.

Summer light;
-streamed church;
'cross meadows.

Flowers in season;
for radiant bride
in walk to altar.

Faces it's written;
recorded delight
at happy day.

Toast and speech.
Then bride called out
"lets' play hide and seek."

Mother said;
"Surely not in
bridal gown?"

"To wear this dress
is only once,"
was bride's reply.

One hundred counted;
house and grounds
were all in play.

Bride went first
to rushing stream,
she knew well.

Lifted slated stone;
A den to hide
when a child.

Slipped beneath,
loud babbled brook;
dressed in gown.

Easy slab
to lift, then;
adult not child.

Down bride went.
Gurgled stream,
drowned out voice.

True hiding place,
that no one new.
Minutes ticked.

Bride had won.
But wasn't found.
House diary said

Gushed water, now
Believed, slab sealed
in mud.

Cries unheard.
Trapped, starved,
not drowned.

A pick opened
cave within.
When culvert dug.

Found beneath;
bride's remains,
scattered floor.

Fingers bitten;
as hunger gnawed;
then curled skeleton.

Skull showed inside,
mice nest fabric,
once bride's gown.

House keeper's
diary gave 1885-
"Bride never found."

Stream has
kept bride's secret,
'til now.

Author embarked on a health training programme to lower cholesterol.

We meet – we part – we meet.

A smile,
sweet recognition.
We meet.
We talk.

'Today, they've
locked you out?'
'Appointments? – "yes,"
but without names.'

"You have to guess,
Who's next;"
time placed, listed,
with no patient name.

Distant in years,
though you share;
admire your acceptance
balance, and calm,
a download that's failed

Scales will tell!
Don't disappoint!
Weeks passed;
Need weight loss!

Banned sweet biscuits,
unnecessary cake;
---walked more, occasional
-but measured drink.

Flow of calories
much reduced.
Seventy grams, no more
in that sweet, yoghurt, pot.

Healthy eating!
+ exercise is good-yes.
Sensible ingredients, advised.
Your tact, charm, beauty;
give added reason to be living.

Sea, pebbles, sand.

Galloping waves,
salt stung eyes;
heat smacked feet;
baked sand.

Young voices
shape the air.
Glee filled delight
at seaside fare.

Deep blue sea;
waves beat to shore;
rhythmic pattern;
bubbled surf.

Slivered seaweed;
rock pool finds;
bucket spaded,
castles built.

Last dash;
final swim.
Next day,
again, the same.
Waves beat
constant rhythm,
falling, rising
on the sand.

Young voices
shape the air.
Glee smiled delight
at nature's fare.

Photos of each
taken on the beach
treasured in
later winter months.
Sand scooped castle
meets the tide.
Seaweed decorates
new daily. build.

From rock pool
then to
castle wall.

A Truth Machine
Automata to supply?

Ride in
our
truth machine.
We'll see the
World in
other vein.
Cross
t's; dot
I's.
Burn
lies
birth
truth.
We'll sight,
spy
perfect statement.
Record
only real.
Wrap up
fake news

Our truth
machine will
dissect ideas
reveal fault
before it
morphs to
matter of fact.
sun rise
and set
that's fact.
it's what
happens
in between
that cooks
primordial
fudge.
Screens
spatter
chatter
palpitates

insists
infallible
world view
Impossibles'
made possible.
Distinct
impossibles'
made plausible
congregation of
Celebrity
entourage
their
tune talk
to media mood.
Exaggeration
supplied
in large spade
to boost
message
multiple.

audiences;
bring bigger
pay pie.
What the heck
make, exaggerate,
scare scenario
from everyday.
To capture
daytime view?
Tell it that way,
they say.
All day
Adjustments,
are to machine
in make
and
patented machine
will
transmit truth,
absolutely?

Autumn

Virginia Vine's
green parade,
turn's scarlet.
Acer's, poignant
red; displays,

crinkled edge.
Stourhead tree;
with brown,
curled leaf.
Bracken drapes:
forlorn, exhausted -
yellow storks.

Hit by gale;
chestnut splatters,
path and road.
Geranium petal,
chilled outdoors;
makes retreat.

Yet, pleasing colours;
musk floored scent,
grass and leaf emit.
Apples, plums,
ripen 'neath,
Autumn sun.

Morning dew,
catches,
spider web.
Signals,
summer
season end.

Autumn harvest;
body-food;
sense in time.

Dreamtime – aspects

Science conjures theory.
Aims to take,
practical reality.

Kinship with
all around,
that owns
its place
and being.
From stone,
to fulsome
Redwood tree.

Peoples harmonized;
that warn of
sickness on and in,
land where
uranium is found.

A culture that
needs embrace
if we wish
to stay alive.
See, scent, hear
know,
life's flow with help
and understand, of
inward, outward, view.

That rainbow
snake gliding
through life's portal;
needs recognition;
and understanding.

Call of the Gulls

For sometimes I do tire
of always and only,
the sway of the seas,
varied mood.

Then do find,
calls from the gull,
music, enough,
for mind,
soul, body.

From memory
wet wretched;
sick: unloved; at
merciless onslaught,
from Sea Tyrant-tress.

Oh gulls, I do
hear you,
who welcome,
each day the sun
that warms the earth,
brings food to your belly.
A sound to fetch a
smile to a sailor,
once, far from land.

A scurry of gulls,
on horizon.

Later, like
gulls, who feed
from a field,
then on land.

Tree

Arterial leaf, drenched,
with moisture flow.
Tendrils, deep in rock and soil.
You, who've snaked
root, ripple
sprawl, in,
man-made meadow;
by a brook.

Hidden
by others,
in a copse.

yet sought,
light, soil, water, space;
many million
years, pre-man,
-virus like,
disrupted earth.

Man: creator of
music word and song;
but sometime
mangler, of how to
get along.

Winter's
grip loosed,

vast map,
buds unwrap,
veined, leaved
canopy;
powerful
oxygen flow.

Air for lungs
and heart.

Seasonal growth,
emits energy burst,
in lives, that see,
each day,
new sunrise.

Heart, life blood.
Earth supply from
tree to man.
A true creative force.
Needs replant;
restoration; replenishment;
writ wide, across earth.

At Home in Lockdown

Longer days,
warmer weather,
allowed one walk.
Trees are near to leaf,
Blossom sprinkles,
here and there.
We enjoy still
Spring fare

It is an episode.
But nature follows
season's path.
Our lives, need,
to find reason,
in appreciation
for home activities,
that once we left,
when outside
and rushed to work –
school, all busy, busy.

Now to listen, not just talk,
With family members,
Who were in
lives;
But more in passing.

Green Growth Escape

City, town,
clad with
spread of
green.

Rain reservoirs
and sculpted
canopy, to
feed
hydroponic
crop in malls.

Vines for wine,
mundane greens
Clematis, Honeysuckle,
Jasmin, climber rose.
Virginia, supervised creeper,
to scale walls.

Horticulture experts,
assist, maintain, construct.
Duty for all to
plant, counter,
air poisoned fume.

Solar energy;
heat for,
berry, salad, veg crop
grown in new purposed,
office build.

Growth in
civic gardens
worked with care.
Oxygenate
grime away.

Reservoir canopies,
catch rain for
plant and flower.

Others, water store,
for hydro turbine flow.

Red, black, white
grape vine, adorn
shopping centre mall.

All those who work,
assist in project,
gifted holiday for
commitment, concern.

Leaf to eat away the
grime, but managed
by all in great
endeavour.
from roof
reservoir turbine
to solar panel cells.

Farmers, nursery garden workers
on community payroll.
Breakaway support
from indoor
occupiers
in supine form
on VDU machine.

Keep full pay, in agriculture
domain of city with "real plant"
described not engineered
man, machine replication.

Cargo Liner – Circa nineteen-sixties.

Laid, sheet plate.
Hull, black riveted;
mainly submerged
redded draft.

Strut of rails;
circle deck;
break, for crew, quarter,
in white, block flat.

Red, black, funnel
Maltese cross;
proud announce;
stands above

Accommodation
block flat, above
main deck.
Green, wedged
tarpaulin hatch;
three forward;
two aft.

Three masts
support
derricks; pulley blocks;
greased wires;
winch engines,
painted green;
dot main deck.

A lifeboat either
Side of funnel deck.
Companionways, run
up, down decks.
Bridge to funnel,
mid deck, main deck.

Outward – Bristol Channel, For Montevideo/Buenos Aires

One, two, three, lower hold
with parcelled
steel plate.
Crates of
car part
agricultural
machinery.
Hospital equipment.
Much more.
Tween decks,
single-decker
Leyland buses;
lorry chassis;
securely wired.

Special cargo lockers.
Wedged casks; unblended
whisky; Drambuie, scotch
whisky, brandy, Gordon's
Gin, all boxed, now stacked
with dunnage to protect.
Railway line;
in lower four-hold;
'Tween-deck
ICI plastic pellets

bagged. Plus,
Leyland buses,
for Buenos Aires
street.

Number five hold;
China Clay bags;
give loads of dust
on load.
Ethanol Drums;
wire lashed,
fore and aft
accommodation
on main deck.

Lorry chassis;
wired secure;
both fore
and after deck.

Return to Bristol Channel from Buenos Aires/Rosario/Bahia Blanca

Mounds of grain;
shifting board
restrained in
holds.

Wool, cotton bales
sling lowered
stacked both
on lower hold.

tween deck -
quality bagged
stacked;
linseed, sunflower
sorghum, cattle feed.

Special cargo lockers;
tween decks,
with canned beef, tongue,
apple, and pear catering can.

Tween deck
No five, salted
cattle skins.
Lower hold
of onions.

Epic Poem: Mists of Time.

A solitary walk down leaf-wrapped lane,
awakened a world, near lost, save now.
 – unexpected presence brought in, revealed;
that farmstead, misted back from
time corridors no longer mine.

Chimney curl of smoke,
above rough-cut grass.
Fence, rambled rose.
Large double-handled
pans, fresh milk steam,
vanished in cold air;
-risen crusts of cream.

Boxes opened,
stacked;
eggs nestled,
laid, in weaved basket.
taken from hedge,
clumped turf, nook
or cranny
near farm door,
found and picked.
Await their inspection;
to be cleaned, sized
boxed, for market.

Across, in view, cobbled,
sloped, bumped, splattered, yard;
tractor, machinery.

That stabled black colt, which bolted.
Grabbed opportunity;
Thro' door opened by me;
it knew I'd lack
real control.

Eyes, senses, mind, recalled;
sixty years past;
activity long absent.
No more, the people
time, nor farm.

Those days, those days,
swapped, switched
for town life then,
to isolated farm.
Quiet, balmy, peace;
escape from family stress.

That, thirteen-year-old,
who baled hay;
swigged rough cider, laced
with orange, whisky.
 – Even got paid!

A smuggled time.
Exploded, capsule;
scented, sounds.
Memory, back-streamed
thro' this canopied leafed lane.

Sketched, hewn, past,
funnelled to me, within arched branches;
informed, refreshed
 – an early memory.
Past, once more revealed;
caught in shaded lane.

Those experiences,
returned, opened once more;
enabled youth recapture,
of unworried world.

––––––––––––––––––––

Before sea, adult life, of
ships, in that wider world.
Fast appreciation met soon;
with farm idyll;
in part only of life's run spool?
Interluded acquaintanceship,
meant so much, then lost, taken back.
Impossible, improbable,
desires – within teen-years.
Young women – more than girls.
Weaved pleasant, smiles, words, looks.
Realistically never to remain – for life's
fierce rush – is not for youth's nonchalance.

Heart knocked blown down'
when their glow
was not love, but
only real for my part.
Warm affection given

with smacked realization, how
young, too young.
They with same age
boyfriend, fiancé,
then to marry;
made good sense in their lives
but, devastation for
one young and foolish.

Training ground for lost affection
with Life's tapestry that can disappoint.
When love is not to be.
That died fierce flame for
one who has left.
All love known
to go – retracted –
split for other –
extinguished –
like day to night.

That-brute bravery,
is then a must;
to meet realities, need;
then each camp site,
one ship, then another.

There a familiar,
meeting place,
acceptance, support given;
when each weight that person pulls;
is interdependent for member crew.

They, who knew, listened, understood;
related to sometime others

indifference; those of land
locked worked, hassled lives
with daily commute.

First shore greets,
belief, perhaps for them, that
world travel,
days at sea, foreign ports;
not real work – against;
theirs of rush and dash to
work and back,
thro' town or city.

Theirs, in perpetuation of
office, factory-with cracked
relentless whip;
demanded presence, response.
Keyboards taped with made screen
electronic blink;
bleeped internet, text, targets, emails,
stale air, fug.

Minutiae of home, flat.
Roof overhead – not ship maintenance.
Wife, children responsibility, care for
immediacy of task in work,
domestic need and home.

Near forgotten, are those teens.
Young years, where self-needs
out-weigh much else.
Before that of crew member, employee,
husband, wife, provider,
who contributes beyond their self.

How wilful, and unforgiving
could that sea mistress be?
To those who respected not;
prepared not;
for raging sea.

A fearful place to
be when fire broke out;
in holds or quarters;
hard to reach and quell.

Habitations of sorrow
still kaleidoscopic back,
into this recall picture.
Marches, far forward
later followed,
absent from that present, time.
Train of memory rush.

A walk, in heaped decades forward.
With remembered farm, now in recall.
Then -part shared in summers,
with those who were always
there – to farm – and be.
Embraced this way,
and stayed.

The generator quiet.
No cows to milk.
No bulbs to light.
No electric supply.
Now broad daylight.
This is what I see
unmisted, out this past.

Framed just awhile for me;
in green canopied lane.

I walk a little further.
But stop for fear like
in a dream this vivid tapestry;
that feeds into my being;
is disturbed and lost.

Then it was that;
two collie dogs sat;
yet jumped to meet, lick, hands, legs.
They far too, friendly, tamed, spoiled
by likes of me, to work the sheep.

A need to stroke each its head, neck, sides;
known that otherwise, one or other
would give whimper of jealous slight.
So fair and true the both.

Clearly remembered – five pears;
clumped, in flowered bowl;
placed to ripen;
purchased that week
from farmers auction –
market of sheep, cattle
orchard produces.

There the auctioneer,
my eye corner caught;
ducked, all but hidden, near parked trailer;
-glugged, whisky bottle swigs;
Dutch courage or just plain addiction?

There was the daughter
of a neighbour farmer's
wedding;
in response, gave relatives, friends evening meal.
Cutlery, plates, electric carving knife,
gifted-then in use.

A matchbox slice of cake to take;
for distant relatives they meet-
-we meet.
There, joy, surrounds, and shares with all.
Fresh, then my eyes to see, feel, that warmth,
joy, happiness.
We'd worked to bring the harvest in.
Now together in joint celebration.

That world caught back
along this walked lane.

———————————

Then transferred to storm
tossed sea;
look out; watches;
holy stoned decks.
Goggles worn to chip
paint, underlying rust;
red leaded; undercoat then gloss.
Green stained brass to rub;
polish mirror clean.
Wheelhouse decks to scrub.

Navigation, seamanship,
Ship construction, science,
English, maths -all to study.

Stapled, chaptered, course sheets.
Struggle to complete – return to marker.
 – Not finished all – before college tutor time.
For test papers;
the Second Mate's exam.

Sea return then followed.
 – To pace that wheelhouse, bridge.
First, a tanker kept in Middle/
far East lands.
Far out from British
Strike bound ports.

Visited by raging fire
in Red Sea, east of Suez.
Crew and ship survived.
Destination Japan.

From hatch – out of sea cadet;
exit was made from
ore carriers, tankers and cargo
liners.

Time ashore for study.
Away from all ships and sea.
Not in contemplative
leafy lanes;
but libraries,
colleges, lodgings or flats.

Out of sea life;
more varied subjects.
Also, female presence,
to entice, distract.

Work found in hotels,
restaurants. But----
new industry strife arrived.
Hotel workers;
union, members met.
Gathered to listen
on beach front.

"More pay, more pay!"
-strike threat ended;
--employers gave
fifteen-pound week - for
hotel waiters, waitresses.

Romance ripped
apart -that work stayed place.
Left in memory time,
for new found love.

A magic spell.
Within a year
-broken,
separated, unglued,
the two of us.

Wounds licked,
Then it was,
to sea front beaches,
promenades,
deck chair ticket sales.

Shared laughter, fun, glee.
A revolved door with change of
steam of holidaymakers,

in those summer weeks.
Then more serious
work to seek.

Interview letters arrive;
 – special need to enthuse,
for companies, most the world
would hardly know.
That at summer's end

Now, no more
sea and ships;
new job venture,
and move to bank
outside London.

Lonesome malaise,
Stifled offices,
frazzled by courses.
Led to disembark.

Return to a
season with
sun, wind salted air;
wind flapped
deck chairs,
beckoned;
before return to
flow of preparation for
interviews and new career.

Manager,
in retail role was that choice.
Not further university study.

Arenas of experience: -
payroll, office, personnel,
fashion, food, cosmetics, clocks, watches;
household goods, shoes,
luggage, curtains.
Fifty-four departments in all.

Ports of the world,
swapped for
towns, city
stores, with sale plans;
expressed in percentage.
weekly figures – "this week,"
"Last week, against "last year."
How much individual weekly sale;
for apples, dresses, curtains,
pork pies or bread?

Store retail life
exited after marriage.
Then with temporary
move to thirty years of
postal work,

There employ
did lead to walks
in leaf strewn lane;
pavements, roads,
towns, village streets.
Postal bags to pack;
trains to meet and
mail bags to dispatch.

Postal retirement from
daily cycle rides.
Much articulated feet and hands-
weight filled letter bags;
then that particular memory-
Farm, sea, ships, banks, sea side
deck chair, hotel, restaurant,
stored, for story recall.
with retail, re-ignited
when shops were
designed fitted, merchandised,
 – opened by eldest son.
Stationery, craft, photo copy,
Merchandising, recruitment of
Work force and managers.
Former retail knowledge restored.
Window displays that
made sales.

Familiar territory,
though locked apart
for thirty years.

Swirled memory mist
now met in walk,
through, canopied, leafed lane.

Why then this bright
life memory,
back in time?

unconscious mind
that choses retrieve
for goals
not yet defined?

Extract Character anthology – fictional – legendary – historical

Achilles. Trojan War Hero

Achilles dipped
by Thetis,
gave protection.
Body, legs, arms;
save where ankles gripped;
perhaps thought lights,
gone out,
dipped so, in that dark Styx.

half-god by mother nymph;
prediction told,
of death heroically.
Disguised son as girl;
hid on Skyros, so -
not to die, glorious warrior.

But this his fate!

Mother sought protection,
with fine armour
Hephaestus wrought
on Isle of Skyros.

Not immortal made.
But all knew;

distinctive strike
of Achille's figure.

King Agamemnon
angered Apollo,
with priest's
daughter taken.

Apollo raged;
sent plague
on Greek army.
One by one
soldiers died.

Agamemnon relented.
Returned same daughter,
for Achilles,
own wife.

Now, Achilles did sulk;
in tent bound anger.
Took armour,
belongings;
stayed put.

This awesome
fighter not in view;
led Trojans,
battle gain.

Patroclus, donned
hero's armour.
Make belief.
Be Achilles.

Apollo,
Seethed,
at priest's
daughter taken;
helped Hector find
and kill Patroclus.

Achilles, hopping mad
slaughtered Trojans;
tit for tat, but
tragic ending,
now likely fact.

Chased Hector
into Troy;
unimpressed
with reason;
killed with
stab in throat.

Hector's plea
for burial honour
dismissed.
Chariot dragged
body to Achaean Camp;
threw on rubbish tip.

Anguished father
pleas for body.
Achille's – gets grief;
his for Patroclus.
Releases battered
corpse to burial.
Attacks Troy still,

for death of friend.
Apollo fired up
in vengeance,
tells Hector's brother
Paris of approach.

Brave warrior,
Paris, not.
Ambush makes.
Apollo guides
Arrow's flight,
to Achille's heel,
undipped in Styx.

Death snatches,
fearless Achilles.
Hero, remaining,
unbeat;
still in battle

Alice

Alice in tumble;
white rabbit pursuit;
dream land,
remembered.
Too tall? Too short?
Pretty garden entry.
Fantasy escape;
Wonder World? Yet-
-highly fraught

Fabled creatures;
confusion;
advice from caterpillar.
Duchess with pepper?
Baby's a pig?
Grinning Cheshire Cat.
Mad Hatter with dormouse,
seeks tea time infinity;
forever on move,
round table.

Cards of status
and none.
Queen of Hearts,
on croquet ground, repeats
"Off with their heads,"
No quarter given;

yet heads stay intact.

Fishy story
from Mock Turtle.
School days that lessened;
Alice with gryphon; explains
Lobster Quadrille.
"Will you walk a
little faster, said a
whiting to a snail…"

Alice's talks
about
fish as food;
retracts, to not
give offence.
Mock turtle
gives Alice
Porpoise
for purpose.

Talk from Alice
of white rabbit;
curious tales;
where more
are to come;
animals remind
Alice of school.
Mock turtle
weeps tears

with song sung;
no upset, after all,
landed turtles,

make tears.
"The trials beginning,"
heard in distance.
A complete pack of cards.
King, Queen of hearts
where king to judge.

Alice finds,
theft of tarts is
now to try.
White Rabbit,
blasts trumpet
for announce.

Mad hatter
there with dormouse;
apologises,
still at tea!
Nonsensical,
like so much.
King gets animal jury
to write tea
dates down.
Execution threatened,
Hatter, in agitation
bites tea cup.

Alice alarmed;
new height growth.
Dispute with
Hatter and King.
Whilst Guinea pigs
Shut out, in act of
suppression.

Hatter keen to
Finish tea.
Keeps head;
exits through
door.

Next witness,
is Duchess –
much sneezing
with pepper.

Dormouse still there;
but thrown out
when "treacle,"
said for tarts.

Confusion follows,
whilst Duchess, cook
also, in disappear.
Alice wonders
Who next witness
Will be…
'til,
White Rabbit
calls out – Alice!!
Dispute arises
over verse;
Jack of spades;
made, but of card.
Alice rushed
by pack;
awakens on sister's
knee.

Vision given
now for sister,
Alice's dream.
White rabbit
Gryphon,
Court room scene
Mock turtle weeping
Swapped for mowing cows.
Elder sister's eyes -
see, Alice, grown woman.
Remembers, wonderland
With small children;
eyes, made bright and eager
told tale now, by Alice.

Arthur

Embedded in our culture,
Welsh and Cornish too,
An awesome leader figure,
that scholars may disown.

Magical and mystical,
We seek to own a truth.
Excalibur the sword;
Arthur came to claim.

That he alone could lead
Brits of yester year
into safety 'gainst,
Saxon foe and fiends.

Sword and scabbard,
with gift of power;
bold imagery of
great leader.

Fabled, that at
round table
1600 men,
could seat.

Of quest for
Holy Grail,
many never
did return.

Sir Galahad,
won the honour,
of attaining
Holy Grail.

Sir Lancelot,
Won love of
Guinevere,
Arthur's fair Queen.

Arthur grew to legend,
saviour of Britain,
from foes then
human & supernatural.

Beloved by his people,
perhaps not as
history seekers
will always like.

Beethoven

Great accolade bestowed.
Composer of all time;
some give Rachmaninov,
as more original.
Genius that no doubt
reached highest level.
Great artist composer;
parallel made to Shakespeare.

Sonatas, concertos,
symphonies and song;
some hearing
believed there,
'til very end.

Said to be difficult.
But then that
part ingredient
might explain greatness
to compose.
Very human
trait excused.

So much to admire,
with wonder
in musicianship.
Composition of broad breadth.
in music resonance.

Great feel, flow
and passion;
subtleties, power, on
percussion.
A repertoire of scores
to give best song,
from human voice.
Phrase from
piano, string,

Faults we could own
of difficult relationships -
with contemporaries of time.
But surely to allow,
awkward squad exception
when such genius exploded,
on music scene, still today.

Forgiven, that
Ludwig, saw in Napoleon,
harmonization
of Europe.
Alas, for disappoint;
but brought Eroica
out of bag,
though emperor
finally locked out
on island.

Timelessly,
Ludwig Beethoven
streams thro'
centuries, with
symphonies, concertos;
sonatas, scores of songs.
Inspires best performance;
conductor, player, singer.
Great reward for those,
who listen.

Boudica

Brutally flogged
and scorned;
daughters raped.
Camulodunum trashed;
slaughtered all and raised to ground.
Marched for Londinium.
Roman divisions fled to Gaul.

Reason for war;
Iceni Queen Boudica
declared – not noble ancestry,
but vengeance for
people's lost freedom;
defiled daughters;
scourged body.
Went on attack,
to avenge all of this.
Men, "may live as slaves,"
It's said, was said;
But she'd not
neglect to
be leader,
in hour of need.

Paulinus regained
Roman province
In desperate battle.
Boudica, queen,

of Britain died
from poison, shock
or illness.

Nero shocked;
abandonment
of unruly land,
real consideration.
Roman records Boudica
 – treacherous lioness.
From Monk Gideer;
Who later named,
Boudica – treacherous lioness.

Slaughter by
Roman conquerors,
enraged these people
with rape of Boudica's
daughters' and flogging
of their queen.
Oppressive Roman force;
that took first their freedom;
then abused their royal house.
Red heated anger made intense.
No quarter given to Camulodunum
slaughtered all and raised to ground
the town.
Rome divisions fled to Gaul.
Britannia victory at Londinium.
Roman revenge followed;
British men, women children;
thousands slaughtered.
Four hundred Romans died;
with slightly larger number injured.

Isambard Kingdom Brunel

Maybe, clockmaker trained
assisted precision, but father started
Isambard with Thames Tunnel.
Collapse led to injury with
lives lost.

Entered design for Clifton Suspension.
But failed on first 'tempt.
Got design through, on second.
Not completed 'til after death.

Not content with tunnels bridges,
went on train and wanted better.
Started work at London/Bristol
Dug tunnel at Box – longest ever.

Multi railway projects.
Rewrote idea for ship capacity.
Two hundred tons of coal, remained,
when Great Western made America.

Completed Thames Tunnel
with shield protection.
Process in use today.
Bridges were his forte.
Many to his name,
But a colossus in engineering.
His works still stand today

So formidable great
person; Isambard
was voted second to,
Churchill, greatest
in all Britain.

Died aged 53 – stroke, but heavy smoker

Part Three: Commentary

Writing routine

Many articles have been written about how important it is to have a routine, with regard to the completion of a project. With a novel, it means pacing yourself through routine, unless you are a writer that can explode with fast flow chapter by chapter through the night and end up with a complete rough draft by the morning? This momentum maybe extended over a week or two and not just a single night. Believe that there will be novelists who have that capacity. This author is restricted not only by typing speed, but also to a more gradual appreciation of where the story is going and reaction from characters A regular two to four o'clock afternoon commitment to writing, has over time seen completion of six novels, two anthologies and a stage play – Persuasion's Price A Play by Sam Grant. Interspersed with deviation into composing poems and short stories, usually at the early stage of a novel. Yet again this is happening while moving a third maritime novel forward!

Once the novel nears the halfway point, then more attention is given, usually, to the extent of early morning, rather than afternoon writing. This, probably due to an appreciation that a first rough draft has becomes a distinct possibility! There can be that hanging around half-way through. Story writers are noted for having a point where the forward movement of plot or story is slowed, at halfway mark.

It has to be that individual writers require to be in their zone. That might be on a computer train, to and from work. The Lockdown of 2020 has not helped, for this writer profile. Mainly, writers will speak of an idyll and reports are given that a certain poet, detective author composed and wrote their best works, in the Lake District or Cornwall, for instance. These reports can be an assumption rather than fact. Experience, is that quite unexpected situations can encourage 'out of the box,' ideas to evolve and that need, is then to write. An idyllic pastoral scene, could become too much of a distraction, this author feels.

There's little doubt that a writing routine is a bonus, in the realm of moving forward. Some days research is needed then writing slows. Research is necessary, but where you are unsure about certain facts it can be best to continue writing but make an underlined note to research later. This may require you, as the author, to make quite large changes, but to begin with, main achievement is completion of a first draft, with all its imperfections!

The real world can intrude. But writing is a real world, you might say – for you! And ten minutes of writing is better than none, when you hope to write normally for two hours, perhaps? A phenomenon can be, that a paragraph written in ten minutes can be the break through toward forward into the story. On return, for a more committed session, better progress is made. Not unlike a play performance, much of the real work is completed before hand. Writing can be the result of an idea, or ideas that have been developing over time. A daily routine of writing does assist in keeping a particular project, like a novel, play, poem or short story on the front burner. A routine disturbed with another writing project does still mean that writing continues. Although, this writer pursues such method, a dedicated professional, in need of meeting a target or targets does need a more disciplined approach to meet deadlines. The fact still remains that routine does establish writing practice which leads to development hopefully, in writing skill overall. Author's first novel was criticized for over use of 'The,' – definite article. This perceived editorial fault, has not prevented novel from receiving good global review, however.

A certain, Chief Officer Geoff Drake had a mantra, which was stated to rookie sea cadets.

"All you need, is an hour and a half of concentrated effort – to learn the morse code." Author Geoff Drake.

Just realized, that this Writing Routine article has similarities in its rule setting down message.

The Play's The Thing

A well-known quote from Shakespeare, "The Play's the Thing." It's reported that Shakespeare composed sonnets and verse when there wasn't much going on elsewhere.

Surmise, that the play would likely be "the thing," when there were bills to pay. Stories brought to life on stage, no doubt would have had wide appeal across social classes, and with a full house, immediate lucrative result.

Author, performed a small part in *Twelfth Night*, at college. What would William Shakespeare have made of our drama teacher's edited version? Before the cast's first read through, we sat down and were instructed to pencil through chunks of spoken actor narrative, which gave an edited version. Maybe? Run time was too long, for time allowed? Also, parents, staff and cadets might not be all that appreciative of lengthy acting parts. Provided an essential story content was there, to maintain audience, attention, all would be well. With large parts, actor cadets at naval college, more able to memorize and cope with revised version of the play? A commentary, reflection about a play author performed in, sixty years, previously.

Would the Bard be dismayed, that fine speeches were abridged to accommodate play run time and specific audience? Author considers, he would likely be up for, play amendment and adaptation, to ensure his play didn't get bad report, from audiences, hat can become restive; to an extent of verbalizing boredom, not only during performance, but afterwards to others, who then would give the play a miss.

Commentary, leads into author Sam Grant's adaptation of *Persuasion's Price, mystery/secret service,* novel into a stage play.

Persuasion's Price – a play by Sam Grant (Colin Coles) has an estimated run time of **ninety minutes,** stage enactment, plus **twenty-minute** interval. A complete run time – **one hour and fifty minutes.**

Once, again play run time might be considered too long by producer/director. Pencil crosses may be order of day. Even where swathes of chapter depiction have been deleted by author, to meet script requirement! It's possible to see how book author might well despair at film director, who cut out parts, seen as integral by author and writer.

Persuasion's Price, mystery thriller, begins in Chapter one, with description of a bullock career escape from a town market. Depiction adapted from memory, of Market Harborough, when author was in role of high street postman.

Bullock escape from town market occurred. In one instance author saw a black and white bullock chase up the high street. Eventually, cornered at top end, no doubt by passer-by who possessed farming skills, in those days of yester year.

Danny, the postman, in *Persuasion's Price,* mystery thriller, is a mix of previously known postal characters from author reflective experience, but not of any one particular person. Postman, women, were known to help farmers with tractor and farm work, in summer season. A postman was noted for scoffing nearly all the biscuits from a biscuit barrel, at a farm coffee stop. The author declares himself – not guilty!

Persuasion's Price is a novel, first published in 2019, in partnership with Paragon Publishing, Rothersthorpe. Suggestive, of earlier postal section rota system. Author, worked while with Royal Mail, at this time, in a four-post person duty team. First duty, was a three-fifteen am run to Leicester to collect mail, for Market Harborough town and village surround, followed by a delivery to a retail park, terminating with the fetch of a second delivery from the train station. Next, a town walk which encompassed the high street on the left-hand side, followed by a delivery to streets that circled into a small retail park delivery before office return. The third and fourth duties were van village deliveries. The third with three village deliveries and the fourth with eight village and hamlet deliveries.

Persuasion's Price, shares fictional reference to the fourth eight village delivery duty, in Market Harborough. Names, are altered, and the novel story is fictional, as are the characters.

Writing topics

Have to admit to answering Quora questions with reservation. That answer is more an opinion than definitive reply. Possibly stimulus arrives to write something positive rather than a diktat about all the mistakes a writer is making in his or her technique.

Lock down, has released a torrent of new novels. Many it appears from media celebrities, who have been unable to perform live. Similarly, to business, an element of luck, is involved when a novel is launched, but perhaps, not to the same extent, when expensive publicity is available for celebrity persons.

Author, has received reader library interest, for his first science fiction novel, *Galactic Mission*.

Where an author's works are available in a few libraries, extent of loans will be limited. First novel, Atlantic Hijack, still achieves sales at book markets. This, has incentivized author, to embark on a third maritime novel. Mike Peter's has elevated to the position of Staff Captain. More passenger characters have been introduced, but novel remains, as a first-person account. A Prologue, main body of work and Prologue has been re-introduced, replicating that of Atlantic Hijack (2015)

Chilling Encounter; this, a third maritime novel, was published in June 2022. Stalled temporarily with diversion to write part two of *Galactic Mission*, which was published in 2020. Also, there has been *Persuasion's Price*, mystery thriller, development into – *Persuasion's Price – The Play*. This absorbed much of 2021's writing time. Publication was in September, 2021.

Several poems are in forge process, prompted, in part of a poetry group, in Frome, Somerset.

Author, Sam Grant, first joined a writing class called Craftyournovel, in 2005, which gave impetus to re-plot and re-write a novel, first named – Pilot's Daughter, which became *Atlantic Hijack*. Poems have been composed, from competition topic ideas, subsequently posted online. A number of poems found their way into *Poems with Themed Notes (2016)* and later *Mists of Time (2018)*

Encouragement arrived when the two maritime novels – Atlantic Hijack and River Escape, received good review from international journal – *Sea Breezes* and latterly copies of *Atlantic Hijack* were requested by British Libraries. In January 2021 the five Book Depository Libraries asked for hard cover copies of *Mists of Time*, to be supplied by the author, through Paragon Publishing, Rothersthorpe. This made up for rejection earlier from author's birth town library of Torquay, who stated that they did not believe there would be interest. Libraries are constrained by the fact that one main supplier provides copies and an author needs to be on this list.

It is though occasional responses from readers, out of the blue, which give resilience to continued new writing projects for author.

Writing and performance art was an interest for author at the age of twenty when Third Mate – no there was no acting involved in the role of watch-keeping officer!

With regard to writing and publishing novels, short stories, poetry and a play fifty plus years forward ambition has become reality.

Retail Wisdom

Author's retailing experience made available for the shopkeeper (former retail trained manager with chain store BHS)

Display and gondola sales

The front end is your prime selling location, followed by the back end. Bestselling positions flow backwards from the front end, either side at middle shelf level. Remember, in general retail and fashion that your premier customers are women. Do not make them have to stretch for your bestselling lines.

Balance and replication are critical factors. When you merchandise front and back ends. Where stock levels permit a complete end to a line can be justified. Strip runs down rather than across each shelf, where a range is displayed. This balance and replication apply equally to window displays. Dressed Mannequins went out of fashion, but shops can accessorize a clothed window mannequin, to good effect. As with all promotions good stock levels need to be instore. Where stock allows create balance replica in a window display. In particular with a fashion or product range – that is the same product at each side of the window – moving inwards with matched colour wither side, to make immediate impact on passers-by. This particularly applies with a large product range, where space allows. Bestselling lines must be given best-selling positions.

Window displays, as mentioned, need to be matched with front end and or good availability, immediately in store.

Window displays, ideally need frequent refreshment, save in exceptional circumstance of ultra-high demand. Before you need to sell from shop window stock, with display collapse a new theme is needed, where good stock levels are there to match display. Plan ahead with your window display. A weekly change, can be hard work , but you do not want to limit your customer base with a stale window display.

Racking

In the nineteen-seventies there was a move by chain stores to do away with window displays. Departmental stores continued with them – arguably they would have been better taking out the windows and replacing with plate glass like the chain stores. A faster paced life style meant that shoppers could more easily see and buy in chain stores, like M&S and Bhs Chain store managements more aggressive selling technique captured a large market share. Sales on a Saturday at the Bhs Broadmead, Bristol store, were in the region of £130,000, in 1972. This needs to be brought into perspective, where a single M&S's store in Marble Arch, purportedly, took in a year, more than all hundred Bhs store chain, across the UK and Northern Ireland.

Practical Application

Again, balance across racking, in particular front displays, is critical, to attract customer interest. Summer season dictates summer fashion and product emphasis at shop front, but weather conditions need to be considered – umbrella racks, rainwear – particularly red, pink and bright coloured fabric brought to store front for impulse purchase. Size and colour coverage are obviously critical to reach across customer choice with rack displays.

Front of store racking is again, most powerful sales position. Second floor sales location, diminishes sales potential for merchandise. Men's fashion, in general retailers, still maintains an upper floor location. Autumn, could, lead to a temporary ground floor display for menswear. Testimony, to the all-powerful sales potential of women's fashion, clothing and lingerie.

Common sense statements, but successful retail demands common sense and a good smattering of flair.

A few tips, from a former chain store manager and latterly manager, within the DTB's # one chain of stationers, across the south west, which translate across retail.

A Beach Swim

A stone's throw from the sea. That was a favourite advertising slogan, in many a guest house brochure or newspaper advert. You might require Olympian and more, throw capacity to achieve stones, projectile needed distance, to validate claim. When author was a child, sea, could be seen from two bedroom, windows. A strip, contrasted with skyline, across fields, dotted pine trees, roof tops and chimney pots. Some days, sea view, from the bedrooms, almost became one, with blue sky.

Three beaches, in walking distance, to invite the swimmer. Meadfoot Beach, farthest away and only became a favourite beach, after sea service. So much can be taken for granted when you live in a town with natural attractiveness. Unappreciated fully with door step availability and before immersion in sea life. There, most shorelines were viewed world ports. Mainly city docks or river jetty, hundreds of miles into Argentina or Venezuela. It is very ill-advised to swim in these rivers, dur to piranha or crocodile. That's apart from, general poor river condition brought about from being a shipping lane.

Meadfoot beach, at time of writing, is a beach littered with fallen rock face and stone debris. When, the tide departs, spots of sand, strewn with seaweed and individual rock pools appear. At further end a pebbly sand beach can be experienced. Anstey Cove, a small rock strewn beach can be reached, by foot, Redgate Beach, adjacent, suffered a rock fall, which cut off beachgoer access by bridge. Farther

along the coast, Oddicombe, had a rock face positioned
dive board, plus pebbled beach, similar to author's romantic
novel. Beach description for – Dancing on the Beach by
Sam Grant. The island, off the beach, is a fictitious creation
for purposes of story.

More recently, in 2021-22, Cleveland Marine Lake has
allowed a return to sea swimming. Not a frequent event, save
in the summer months, although author's eldest son has been
known to complete four to six lengths at a time. Wet suits are
worn, but water warms in the summer months, sufficiently
not to feel need of a wet suit. Water can be murky, for this
man-made lake, over run by incoming high tides. Water
clarity influenced by river estuary and tidal wave capacity. A
dive in approach, as from boat or ship, is not an option. The
Marine lake barely above waist height front near sea side.

No choice, other than to dangle legs into the lake and
summon up the courage to lower yourself down. While
crowd-viewed by seagulls, either wheeling above or stood on
lake's far wall barrier. Perhaps, sat there in contemplation
of a supermarket type promenade foray, after discarded fish
and chip carton; dough nut remnant, dropped splodged
cornet cone or similar delicacy. They do seem to look
contemptuously, over, and might even have stopped from
food hunt spree, to spectate, this land creature's attempt to
overcome fear of full impact with cold water. Impetus, to
forward driven by appreciation that to stand waist height
without movement has chilled lower body, and activity is
needed or you might as well leave the lake. One method,
is to pretend, kid yourself, that most cold effect has been
accommodated by lower half already being immersed. That
possibly less than half your body, remains above the lake.
"Anyway," you came to swim – didn't you? Tell yourself, to

get on with it! A breeze across the lake that further chills your upper body and arms, can be a deciding factor in which a plunge is made, followed by vigorous strokes toward the middle. An immediate "isn't it cold moment," made less intrusive, if you tell yourself that it must have been that much colder back in April. How we like to make comparison, in the belief that a situation sees improvement, over time.

Also, that susceptibility to an expert's advice. Dr Mosely has recommended that two rapid exercise pedals, with short rest in between is more effective and health improving than just the one alone. Two swimming sessions, spaced with a short rest in between the two has been completed on swim visits to the Marine Lake, by author.

Free will, Choice, Coincidence

Scientifically conducted tests, have projected coincidence to be not that unlikely, but probably we can all recall exceptional events that we would say are something more than coincidence?

Apparently meeting up with someone you knew ten or more years ago in a different town, is according tom this theory of non-coincidence not exceptional.

Author, sort of runs with conclusion, as a seafarer working aboard ships for a shipping company there could be regular meet ups with seafarers known aboard other ships, but it can be said some coincidental meet ups can have degree of spookiness.

Unusual words can have a habit of being not that unusual on a particular day. In fact nearly everyday, in author's recollection. An early day reading of a word like poignancy, tenacity, tremulous, synchronicity, to suggest a few, read in a book in the morning and then the word is spoken by a news person, television presenter or maybe on the radio in the afternoon. The duplicate occurrence of these words is given the marker of not that unusual by science appreciation? But with author's principles of navigation seafaring background, whereby position is made by intersection on a chart with dot position which is very accurate, could it be with words there is some kind of position intersection at work? Best to leave it there perhaps.

How much control do we have as individuals over memory experiences, which might inform later decisions, unknowingly. Even with regard to colour choice, where repeated visual experience to specific shade, within specific colours, might impact and disallow us true freedom to decide?

The End

Other Books by the author

Please check out these other publications by the same author.
Follow blogs, poems and stories at
Samgrantpublications.wordpress.com
Sam Grant, Author – Facebook.

Atlantic Hijack (978-1-78222-291-0); *Action, mystery; Sea adventure in the South Atlantic*
A secure orderly passage aboard a cargo liner is ripped apart by a brutal terrorist attack.
River Escape (978-1-68222-574-4); Sequel to *Atlantic Hijack*. *Action, mystery*
Venezuela: An oil terminal in the River Orinoco, Venezuela. Following on from a military coup. Mike's pressured efforts to prepare the tanker for the load of boiler oil are compromised by a refinery postponement.
Dancing on the Beach (978-1-78222-431-0); *Romantic thriller*
Phillip Norton obtains summer work as a deckchair attendant and soon he is into a heady romance with the receptionist.
Persuasion's Price (978-1-78222-687-1); *Mystery thriller*
A quiet market town in England is shattered by an explosive mix of gang rivalry and shady deals.
Persuasion's Price – The Play (978-1-78222-870-7)
Play, in ten acts. Includes full script and stage instructions ready for rehearsal.
Galactic Mission (978-1 78222-512-6); *Science fiction*
It is 2110, QUADRANT is the world government. But the world is not at ease and relationships are put under strain. James Walters encounters Adriana – "The Empress Adriana" – from the Galactic Command Force.

Galactic Mission Part Two (978-1-78222-773-1);*Science fiction,* sequel to Galactic Mission
In this classic sci-fi adventure, the main characters from Galactic Mission, including the Empress Adriana, are working to divert comets away from Earth by firing a missile from Mars.

Poetry and short story publications by Sam Grant
Poems with themed notes (978-1-78222-464-8)
Love Starved by Electronics is a sonnet selected for a 'Sonnets for Shakespeare' anthology.
In *Riding Through Time* ghostly horsemen appear to ride down the ages. *Captured into their Realm* – a meeting with an alien depicted in verse. *Eye of the Storm; The Time Makers Kingdom; Thankful Thoughts* and *Spirit of Spring.* These are a few of the poems in this varied anthology.
Mists of Time (978-1-78222-708-3)
From epic poem to scary short story, *Mists of Time* entertains and enlightens. In the title poem, author Sam Grant takes us on a journey. Perhaps his journey, down a leafy lane to a farm in summer, off to sea and beyond. *Secret Cave* is a short story informed by a love of sail boat sailing, a reflection from the author's young life, before the author embarked on a career in the Merchant Service.
Part One – Poems both in traditional and modern form. Dramatic, but also light-hearted topics explored.
Part Two – Short stories.
Individual cameo chapters.

Sam Grant, Author

URL *amazon.com/author/grantsam*
samgrantpublications.wordpress.com

Ingram Content Group UK Ltd.
Milton Keynes UK
UKHW020610280623
424104UK00012B/382